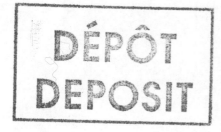
Integrating all young people into society through education and training

Volume 1

Proceedings of the meeting

Brussels, 7 and 8 May 1998

EUROPEAN
COMMISSION

A great deal of additional information on the European Union is available on the Internet.
It can be accessed through the Europa server (http://europa.eu.int).

Cataloguing data can be found at the end of this publication.

Luxembourg: Office for Official Publications of the European Communities, 2000

Volume I: ISBN 92-828-7632-2
Volume I and II: ISBN 92-828-7630-6

Printed in Italy

PRINTED ON WHITE CHLORINE-FREE PAPER

Preface

In the European Union between 10 to 20 % of young people leave the education system without any qualifications at all, while 45.5 % of young people aged from 15 to 24 have only low-level qualifications; at best having completed lower secondary school education. With no qualifications or basic skills, their career prospects are bleak.

The White Paper on growth, competitiveness and employment stressed that developing education and training is one of the prerequisites for a new model of economic growth that will create jobs. Education and training also lay the foundation for citizenship and social cohesion.

On the basis of this analysis, the White Paper 'Teaching and Learning — Towards the Learning Society', adopted by the European Commission in 1995, emphasised the importance, in building this European Union of knowledge, of paying particular attention to those sections of the population experiencing the greatest difficulties, i.e. young people in particular.

The Treaty of Amsterdam gave the European Union new powers in the area of employment. The main conclusion of the ensuing 'Luxembourg' process was that addressing the problem of school dropout rates and under-achievement at school should be one of the guidelines for employment policy. All the Member States have incorporated this issue in their national employment plans.

Directly inspired by the guidelines proposed in the White Paper (third general objective: combat exclusion), DG XXII (Education, Training and Youth) has taken two initiatives to actively prevent exclusion.

Firstly, the Commission, in conjunction with the governments concerned, is providing support for a series of pilot 'second chance school' projects. Over the past two years, around 10 second chance schools have been set up in various Member States. They were carefully selected out of around 100 spontaneous applications from European cities and regions.

The specific characteristics of each school depend, to a large degree, on national and local conditions. However, all the projects have two characteristics in common: strong local partnership with employers in particular, and an integrated and individualised educational approach in which centre stage is given to acquiring skills in and using new technologies.

Secondly, the Commission, in line with the wishes of the Member States and the European Parliament, has sought to link up all the ongoing national initiatives and ensure that the maximum advantages are reaped from these projects.

Each Member State has implemented various provisions and measures to prevent exclusion among young people, tailored to its particular national and regional requirements.

With a view to the setting-up of this 'second pillar', the Commission organised, on 7 and 8 May 1998, a conference bringing together over 160 representatives of different national and local bodies working in the area of social exclusion.

This conference succeeded in demonstrating the richness and diversity of the Member States' various measures and initiatives to foster the educational, social and occupational integration of young people. They ranged from workshop schools in Spain to production schools in Denmark, from recurrent education in Portugal to regional training centres in the Netherlands.

The Commission has great pleasure in presenting the proceedings of this conference. They include the complete texts of the speeches made by the political decision-makers, experts and practitioners, the conclusions of the various thematic workshops, and a brief description of each of the projects covered during the conference.

This conference provided an opportunity to put the issue of social exclusion among young people back at the heart of political debate. It provided a timely reminder of our knowledge-based society's responsibility towards citizens experiencing difficulties in acquiring the skills and qualifications required in today's world.

My hope is that this publication will allow each and every one of us to renew our commitment to preventing and remedying social exclusion, which threatens to waste this knowledge-based society's most precious asset: its human resources.

Domenico Lenarduzzi
Deputy Director-General
Education and Culture Directorate-General

Foreword

This record of proceedings of the conference 'Integration of all Young People into Society through Education and Training', which was organised by the European Commission on 7 and 8 May 1998, gives an overview of both its contents and the participants.

Volume 1 presents the actual texts of the different contributions, which fall into three main categories:

- The 'political' part contains the contributions on the policy challenge posed by the problem of social exclusion in general and the social exclusion of school dropouts in particular. The papers presented provide a well-balanced range of viewpoints from the European Commission, the Social and Economic Committee, the Committee of the Regions, as well as those of a 'case study' Member State (Germany in this instance).
- The 'analytical' part looks at three studies conducted under the Socrates programme. The three experts who addressed the conference highlighted the educational, social and statistical significance of school failure and gave a comprehensive overview of both prevention and remedial strategies, illustrating 'good practice' with examples from within and from outside the formal education systems.
- Finally, the workshops allowed participants to focus their discussions on six main issues common to all projects: pedagogic innovation, the role of new technologies, the problem of validation and certification of skills, the requisite qualifications for teachers involved in second-chance initiatives, the involvement of employers in these schemes and, last but not least, the importance of local partnerships. The third part of Volume 1 thus includes six sub-chapters, corresponding to the themes of the workshops, in which the texts of the different contributions, as well as the workshop conclusions, are presented.

Volume 2 is a collection of short analytical presentations of the different conference contributions. These are concise rather then exhaustive, but nonetheless give the reader an idea of the wide range of tentative action being taken in the EU in the endeavour to stem social exclusion. The European Commission indeed made painstaking efforts to ensure that the group of conference participants be as representative as possible of European practice in this field. The national ministries of education and/or social affairs, as well as the European education network Eurydice, were involved for this purpose — and the three experts mentioned above succeeded, under the Socrates studies programme (Action 3.3.1), in identifying worthwhile examples of good practice in this broad and multidimensional policy field.

Full particulars of contact persons are provided should any reader wish to seek further information or, indeed, to propose joint projects at European level.

Although this publication is strictly speaking the record of a conference at which the participants represent only a fraction of the very wide range of social integration projects across the EU, the reader will appreciate that the problems raised and the solutions proposed provide for a very valid global assessment of the stakes in the fight against social exclusion in Europe. Whilst every Member State — and indeed, every locality — faces its own unique set of policy challenges and options, the conference has succeeded both in elucidating the common denominator in this wide range of initiatives and in stating the case for cooperation at European level.

The Commission's capacity to support such European cooperation will shortly get a significant boost under the new Education and Training programmes which are likely to come on stream in January 2000.

There will be greater emphasis both in the new 'Grundtvig' action of the Socrates II programme and in the Leonardo da Vinci II programme on transnational exchanges for social and educational reintegration initiatives.

We should like to thank all conference participants for their interesting contributions to the discussions. We also take this opportunity to invite other readers to become part of this growing circle of 'second chance' protagonists.

European Commission
Directorate-General
Education and Culture

The 'Second Chance Schools' team,
Anders J. Hingel
Edward Tersmette
Fabienne Bessonne

Contents

Introduction

Between 10 and 20 % of young people in the European Union leave the education system without recognised qualifications and 45.5 % of 15 to 24-year-olds have only low-level qualifications: at best the lower secondary certificate. This lack of qualifications and basic skills severely limits their participation in civic life and their prospects of finding work.

The White Paper 'Teaching and Learning: Towards the Learning Society', adopted by the Commission at the initiative of Mrs Édith Cresson and Mr Pádraig Flynn, stressed that we need to construct a Europe of knowledge on which we can draw in order to improve the situation of those groups facing the worst hardships, in particular young people.

For their part, all the Member States have implemented a wide range of measures and systems to combat exclusion that reflect their own specific features and are in some cases supported by Community initiatives and programmes. Much has been achieved, in some cases with remarkable success about which often too little is known. A much broader range of training, in which the key player is again the student, is now available. Closer links have been forged between schools and enterprises enabling them to work together in better ways, and programmes for young people aged between 16 and 25 have been implemented.

DG XXII 'Education, Training and Youth', in response to the objectives set out in the White Paper (Objective 3 'Combating exclusion'), has stepped up this fight against exclusion in two ways. On the one hand, the Commission is supporting, in agreement with the governments concerned, a set of pilot 'second chance school' projects. On the other hand, the Structural Funds (especially the European Social Fund) and the Socrates and Leonardo da Vinci programmes (for education and training respectively) have provided a framework for innovative social and occupational integration projects. The European Voluntary Service is also offering young people an opportunity to benefit from new training experiences abroad while also assisting local development.

In parallel with these pilot projects, we need to build on the wealth and diversity of local, national and Community measures and to promote transnational exchanges and cooperation projects in order to build on their results, pinpoint those aspects that can be transferred and pave the way for new experiments.

This kind of strategy makes it possible to focus the debate on young unemployed people, while bearing in mind that prevention is a necessary strategy that complements re-integration. This conference therefore looked at dropping out from and failure at school and pinpointed good practices that help to prevent failure at school and that use education and training to integrate young people into employment and society.

Objectives

This conference therefore had three objectives:

- to review, in detail, the forms and causes of failure at school;
- to bring together significant examples of education and training measures that have been successful in integrating those young people facing the worst hardships, whether implemented by Member States, local authorities (regions, provinces or towns), enterprises or training agencies, whether or not these measures were part of a Community initiative;
- to promote transnational exchanges of experience and cooperation projects within a network infrastructure supported by the Commission.

The conference provided an opportunity to bring together European experts on school, social and occupational integration, to compare completed or ongoing experiments, to provide a forum for experts and politicians to discuss what measures are needed for the successful integration of disadvantaged young people and to sketch out ways of networking these educational experiments at European level and the content of such a network.

Part I

Combating failure at school:
The political challenge

Opening of the conference

Mrs Édith Cresson,
Member of the Commission

It is with great pleasure that I open this conference on the social and economic integration of disadvantaged young people through education and training. The fight against the exclusion of young people is as close to my heart as it is to yours.

A few figures illustrate the situation of disadvantaged young people in the European Union:

*   some 15 % of 15 to 24-year-olds are not in employment or education;
*   45 % of them leave school with a lower secondary certificate at best;
*   only 56 % of those who left school with few qualifications have jobs in comparison with 74 % of other young people;
*   in this age group, 39 % of under-qualified young people, i.e. 3.3 million people, risk exclusion from the labour market (according to Eurostat criteria). The situation of these young people varies: they are employed under precarious conditions, they work part-time because there was no other option, they are unemployed, etc.

To gain an accurate picture of the problem, we need to add in all those young people who currently have jobs but are at risk because of their lack of qualifications.

Lastly, according to a Eurobarometer survey in 1994, three million young people feel completely excluded and 41 million partially excluded. These young people feel that the main cause of their exclusion is the poverty of their parents. They also feel that education is the best way of fighting this exclusion.

These statistics speak for themselves. On their own, they provide, however, only part of the picture. For a true picture, we need also to look at what these young people are saying: they are all telling us that they are willing but disillusioned, that society does not seem prepared to accept them, and that they find it difficult to imagine what the future holds for them.

The European Commission's White Paper on teaching and learning: towards the learning society, adopted in November 1995, sets out five general objectives for European action. I should like to recall them briefly:

*   encouraging the acquisition of new skills,
*   forging closer links between schools and enterprises,
*   mastery of three Community languages,
*   placing tangible investment on a par with investment in training,
*   combating exclusion.

It is with this final objective in mind that I have proposed to set up, with the agreement of the governments concerned, what are being called 'second chance schools' for unqualified young people.

These are based on three principles:

*   In the first instance, considerable flexibility, enabling each young person to construct, with the help of a mentor and in cooperation with local employers, his or her own training route. This route will take account of each person's needs and expectations as well as his or her skills. We should not forget that

these young people have skills which, even though they have not been validated by the educational system, can help them to regain a positive image of themselves.

- Then, an integrated approach that covers all these young people's needs: not just education and training, but health, accommodation, administrative problems, etc. This requires a multi-disciplinary team and a strong partnership between the various local partners involved: social services, associations, etc. Enterprises play a key role in this partnership because they are involved in the scheme from the outset: formulating training routes and pinpointing what skills are required on the local labour market, making mentors and training places available in enterprises and, when this training has been completed, recruiting these young people.
- Lastly, these second chance schools mobilise high-quality and innovative educational resources that make use of the new technologies and call on experienced teachers, educators and mentors.

Over and above these three basic principles, each project adopts the profile that is best in keeping with its political, social, economic and cultural environment. The institutional form of the 'school', its size, the methods by which young people and trainers are recruited and its strategy as regards enterprise consequently differ from one location to another.

The following locations have so far been chosen: Marseilles in France, Bilbao and Barcelona in Spain, Catania in Italy, Nikea near Athens in Greece, Seixal in Portugal, Hämeenlinna in Finland, Ribe in Denmark, Heerlen in the Netherlands, Halle and Cologne in Germany, Leeds in the United Kingdom and Norrköping in Sweden. Representatives of these projects are attending this conference and you will have an opportunity to meet them.

We should not forget, however, that the integration of disadvantaged young people is a fight in which the governments of Member States and many other partners: local authorities, associations, etc., have long been involved.

It is for this reason that we feel it important to provide a discussion forum for all these partners. The diversity of education and training systems in the Union and the wide range of experiments that have been conducted provides a wealth of information on which we can draw to promote high-quality education and training for these disadvantaged young people. The major challenge that this integration work poses means that every possible step has to be taken to improve the quality and efficiency of existing schemes, that we need to keep ourselves informed to stimulate creativity and that we must be open to innovation.

I should like to cite three of the many examples of innovative schemes represented here:

- The workshop schools of Gijon in Spain which are part and parcel of a job-creation scheme for disadvantaged young people and which train them in trades connected with the rehabilitation of the cultural, natural and industrial heritage.
- An Internet café project in Montabaur in Germany whose aim is to provide a meeting place for disadvantaged young people and to help them to analyse their skills and needs and then to take part in training in the new IT trades ('info-broker' or computer recycling, for instance).
- A Finnish project 'My Own Career', which is aimed at secondary school pupils who have failed at school or who are at risk of exclusion. This project takes an approach which is both global and individual and is intended to motivate these young people and to develop their personalities so that they can construct a personal plan (taking part in adventure camps, discussion forums, meetings with representatives of various institutions, etc.).

Over these two days, you will have an opportunity to exchange experiences and to talk about the main problems that you face.

After this conference, we invite you to pursue these exchanges and to forge cooperation links. Teaching methods, the development of new teaching aids, the training of teachers and trainers and the use of the new technologies are all subjects for cooperation. This cooperation may also provide an opportunity for the young people, for whom and with whom you work, to expand their horizons, to talk with other young Europeans and jointly to formulate new projects, as some of you are already doing.

I hope that you enjoy two days of fruitful work and meetings.

Opening address

Karl-Johan Lönnroth
Director, DG V
Employment, Industrial Relations and Social Affairs

Mr Chairman, Distinguished Commissioner Cresson, Colleagues, Friends, Ladies and Gentlemen

I am very honoured to have the opportunity to address this conference today. Not only is the integration of young people into society a key topic on the European agenda. As a representative of DG V, responsible for employment, industrial relations and social affairs, I wish also to emphasise that we work hand in glove with DG XXII inside the Commission to address this problem, and thereby contribute to make Europe a better place for the citizens to live and work in. I have no reason to doubt that these mutually supportive actions are also undertaken by the different actors concerned at the level of the Member States.

My intervention will focus on two broad issues:

1. the key role of employment in the European construction and the importance of the inclusion of young people in this respect; and
2. the way the European Social Fund is linked to the European employment strategy, and how the Agenda 2000 reforms can enhance its efficiency in promoting a high skill European Society.

I would like to recall the four major 'construction sites' we have in Europe at the moment:

1. the EMU and the completion of the single market,
2. the development of the European employment strategy,
3. enlargement, and
4. the reform of the financial framework and the related European instruments to promote cohesion in the widest sense of social and economic cohesion.

In a sense, employment cuts across all of these construction sites. If employment is considered as the most effective social policy, and the best means of social inclusion and access to well-being, then the provision of more and better employment and access to the world of work for all who want it becomes a crucial test of success of all of the above construction programmes.

The inclusion of young people into society in general and into the labour market in particular is an important element of this challenge posed by the construction of Europe.

The problems in this respect are well known:

1. Out of a total of 18 million recorded as unemployed, nearly 5 million are young people under 25, that is 10 % of the population aged 15 to 24.
2. For EU as a whole, young people's unemployment rate (21.8 %) is twice as high as adults' unemployment rate and in some MS, the unemployment rate of young people under 25 is even three times as high as the adults' unemployment rate.
3. Nearly two thirds of unemployed young people have been out of work for more than 6 months and 40 % for over 12 months.
4. Even when they have access to jobs, young people tend to have increasingly precarious jobs either temporary contracts or part-time jobs. This reflects both lack of job-opportunities and changing production patterns of the economy, but also changing attitudes towards work and career development.

Policies which aim at coming to grips with these problems have both an economic and a social rationale: not only is youth exclusion and unemployment an enormous economic waste. If we look at the future, the economic rationale is even clearer: Ten years from now, 80 % of the technology used today will be obsolete. At the same time, almost 80 % of the work force will not possess the skills and knowledge that the new technologies require. Newly educated young age groups will potentially be among the 20 % who do, if our training and educational systems are capable of providing them with the required skills and required preparedness for the working life.

But 10 years from now we will have 9 % fewer young age groups on the labour market, while the work force is ageing and the total growth of the labour force is approaching zero. This means that we need the productive capacity of everyone to keep Europe competitive and to meet the financial burden that the demographic change imposes on our pension, health and social protection systems. We can neither afford to have a policy which puts different age groups in competition with each other on the labour market, nor can we afford letting groups at risk drift into exclusion and oblivion.

Furthermore, the social exclusion of young people also has its social dimension. We know that exclusion becomes a generational problem for the individual, which will haunt her throughout the lifetime making her less competitive and less adaptable for change. And we know that exclusion carries with it spillover effects related to urban decay, criminality, and the degradation of the social tissues.

We know that the problems I have cited are partly due to our own incapacity in Europe to handle macro-economic shocks of the last 25 years in a coordinated way and our inability to reform our labour market and our social protection systems to meet the needs of the labour market of today, which has led to the present poor job creation and low employment rate. But they are partly also due to the insufficient ability of our education and training systems to anticipate and cope with the requirements of structural change and the needs of labour market.

Despite substantial and steady progression of the participation rates in education and training, despite the growing importance of vocational education and training in most MS, there are still too many young people who leave education and training systems without recognised marketable qualifications: around 10 % young people in Europe drop out of school early, too early to acquire any qualification and around 45 % leave school before reaching upper secondary level.

Despite important efforts made by MS to improve or extend their vocational education and training, VET is still less valued than general education and the capacity of VET to follow the changes of the world of work is too low.

All too often, education and training systems map out career paths on a once-and-for-all basis. There is too much inflexibility, too much compartmentalisation of education and training systems. This is adapted neither to the need of modern economies and societies which request a high level of adaptability nor to young people who do not respond to barriers, to fixed paths and want instead exciting possibilities, bridges between courses, training paths, a range of options and choices.

We want to construct a European society which is based on equal opportunity, social inclusion, high skills and high levels of employment — all of these principles being part of the European social model. This is why the Amsterdam Treaty assumes particular significance for the issues we are about to discuss today.

The development of high quality human resource is addressed at the very beginning of the new title on employment in the Amsterdam Treaty in its first article (Article 125) which establishes the promotion of a skilled, trained and adaptable workforce as one of the areas for the coordinated strategy together with employment and the promotion of labour markets responsive to economic change. This clearly makes education and training issues a central element of the debate and of the policies.

The Treaty, by stating that employment is a matter of common concern, also implies that employment should be taken into account in the design of all Community policies, including those related to education and training.

The Treaty has, therefore, created a completely new situation in the European Union in the field of employment policy. It has not only brought employment and social policy to the centre stage of policy-making, on an equal footing with macroeconomic and fiscal issues. By receiving the political endorsement, that the employment provisions should be implemented immediately, the Amsterdam Treaty is at the origin of the 'Luxembourg process'. This process was launched at the European Jobs Summit in Luxembourg last November. The 'Luxembourg Process' is, first, a convergence process, where Member States have committed themselves to converge towards higher levels of employment.

It is, secondly a country surveillance process, where Member States have submitted themselves to a yearly scrutiny of their performance and to an exchange of best practice.

It is thirdly, a management by objectives approach, where Member States have agreed to set quantified targets for their policy, without which success and failure could not be assessed and a peer review not be possible.

The centrepiece of the new Luxembourg process is the adoption of yearly Employment Policy Guidelines which is similar to the Broad Economic Policy Guidelines, and the subsequent drawing-up of National Action Plans for employment, which should translate the Employment Policy Guidelines into action at the level of the Member States — which remain responsible for employment policy. The Treaty also foresees recommendations to individual Member States adopted by qualified majority by the Council, which was not possible before.

The Employment Guidelines identify four pillars of the European strategy for employment, which constitute the four main lines of action for the MS: improving employability, developing entrepreneurship, encouraging adaptability in business and for their employees, strengthening the policies for equal opportunities.

We are now at the point of finalising the examination of the first National Action Plans delivered by all Member States at the end of April to the Commission, along the lines agreed and on the basis of the first Employment Guidelines adopted in December 1997. The analysis will be adopted by the Commission next week and submitted thereafter to the European Council in Cardiff in mid-June.

I am not in the position today to give you an account of the full content of the Member States' responses to the Guidelines and the Commission's assessment of them. It is, however, clear that as the favourable economic prospects underpinned by a track record of years of stability oriented macroeconomic policies have now created high expectations for sustained employment growth, which might reach 8.5 million new jobs by the year 2002. The Member States focus strongly on the development of labour supply to increase the skill levels and to make labour force adaptable to change, thereby avoiding bottlenecks and strengthening the job content of growth.

The guidelines as such imply a breakthrough in the level of commitment to training and to the development of Europe towards a learning society. Training is a key element in a number of the guidelines, especially as regards young people, such as: preventing the drift into long-term unemployment by requiring the provision of a new start for every young person before the unemployment reaches six months, requiring the social partners to agree on increased training provision and to open up the work places, i.e. for traineeships, reducing substantially the number of school dropouts, equipping young people with skills relevant for the new labour market, developing apprenticeship training, increasing overall training provision for the unemployed from the current European average of less than 10 % examining obstacles to and providing fiscal incentives for enterprise training.

In fact virtually all of the 19 guidelines adopted at the European level require measures which benefit the inclusion of young people, and the Member States have indicated a host of measures and initiatives to meet these objectives. The Luxembourg process implies, therefore, a quantum leap in the European efforts to meet the employment challenge.

The European Social Fund is an important instrument to support the Member States in this process. This conference has, therefore, a particular interest in the Social Fund, as the main EU instrument in the education and training field. Agenda 2000, and the reforms of the European Structural Funds will, if adopted, enhance the possibilities of underpinning that strategy in a simpler, more efficient and more transparent framework. This will be a case of one plus one makes three: the Social Fund will provide the strong financial underpinning for the employment strategy, while the policy impetus provided by the Employment Strategy will reinforce the impact of the Social Fund on good practice and innovation.

I would now briefly like to outline the role the Social Fund occupies within the overall scheme and highlight the key changes which I consider to be important.

Central to this is the role of Objective 3. The basic aim of this new Objective 3 is to support the adaptation and modernisation of policies and systems relating to education, training and employment. In financial terms, Objective 3 will operate outside the areas concerned by Objectives 1 and 2, but it is vital to understand that it will also serve in each Member State as a policy frame of reference for all Funds activity in human resources development.

Secondly, I would like to stress the increased emphasis on policy development. We are looking for new partnerships with Member States around new strategic developments and innovations in our education and employment systems, bringing structural fund assistance to bear on new goals and ambitions.

As a result, and given the seven-year life-span of the new regulations, the eligible measures have been quite broadly defined so that we can dovetail the assistance provided and the National Action Plans for employment. This should ensure that the funding is appropriate to the national and regional priorities and policies of each Member State.

Our draft regulation proposes five general policy fields in which the ESF will intervene:

(i)   Active labour market policies to fight unemployment.
(ii) Promotion of social inclusion.
(iii) Promotion of employability via lifelong education and training systems.
(iv) Anticipation and facilitation of economic and social change.
(v)   Equal opportunities for men and women.

This is a mix of the old and the new, a package of the main concerns facing employment and human resource policies in the next period. Given the particular interest of this conference, I will not go into detail about the fields as a whole, but I will say something about what we expect to be done under the 2nd field, that of social inclusion.

Here, we are inviting Member States to use the ESF as part of their fight against discrimination of all sorts in accessing the labour market. The ESF is a labour-market-oriented fund – so naturally it cannot take on the whole issue of exclusion; but it will work, for example, through pre-vocational measures – recognising that many of those excluded from employment now cannot be expected to integrate at once, but will need help in getting back closer to working life. Indeed, here the whole concept of the 'pathway to integration', the individualised map charting the way back into working life, is one which the ESF has championed across all Member States, and with excellent results.

The new regulations also enable Member States to use the Fund for other sorts of accompanying measures, such as all forms of guidance, or even the provision of child-care, essential to many would-be working women for whom paying for child care is out of the question.

It is not for the Commission to instruct Member States as to which projects should be supported – in the decentralised arrangements which I have described, that is for those nearer the ground than we. But there is certainly much scope for supporting initiatives like the Second Chance Schools in this context, as an interesting example of how to reach out to disadvantaged young people and bring them back into the mainstream of working life.

It remains for me now to hope that this conference will provide an important contribution to the further development of the European employment strategy, distil new ideas for the inclusion of young people in the world of work, and come up with useful proposals as to how the Social Fund can assist in meeting this challenge.

Thank you for your attention.

Action on the integration of young people

Dr John Evans
The Committee of the Regions (UK)

I propose to start by outlining the role and purpose of the Committee of the Regions and then to indicate our views on the integration of young people and our role in this vitally important work.

The Committee of the Regions (COR) is composed of 222 elected members from across all the European Union Member States. Our role is twofold, firstly to act as a voice for local and regional government within the EU and secondly, to express our opinion on EU legislative proposals or policy orientation documents emanating from the Council of Ministers or the European Commission.

Our legal status is enshrined in the Treaty of Maastricht and this is due to be enhanced to include consultation by the European Parliament when the Treaty of Amsterdam is endorsed by all of the Member States.

We are organised into several subject commissions according to the specific competences of local and regional government. The commission of which I am a member is Education, Vocational Training, Culture, Youth, Sport & Citizens' rights. Quite clearly the integration of young people is a matter of vital concern to us all. It is also well within the specific remit of all local and regional authorities across the EU. That is why we accepted the invitation to make this intervention at the conference — and I wish to offer my congratulations to DG XXII especially, for the initiative in calling this conference and for my small part within it.

The COR has strongly supported the integration of young people into society in the recommendations it has made in many of its opinions. For the COR, this concerns not only integrating young people into the labour market but also into social, cultural and civic life. We believe that education and training are positive tools which can discourage alienation, racism, xenophobia and violence by promoting tolerance, solidarity and participation in the democratic decision-making process and participation in the cultural and social life of their communities. This role should not be overlooked.

Recently the COR has focused on the issue of improving employability and improving employment opportunities through education and training in its work on the role of local and regional authorities in the EU in linking education and training establishments to enterprises. This work has shown that education and training systems are very often developed in total isolation from the enterprise environment and labour market demands of a locality or region, despite the fact that growth, competitiveness and employment prospects of an area are increasingly dependent on the skills of its current and future workforce.

The COR has, therefore, underlined the need to step up cooperation between both sectors through local and regional networks and has called for support to be given to local and regional partnerships and for the dissemination of best practice on how to develop those partnerships across the EU. In recognition of the value of promoting the exchange information in this field, the European Commission will be organising together with the COR and the local hosting locality/region, a series of seminars on local and regional experiences linking education and training establishments to enterprises.

It is the COR's view that: closely connected as they are with the area's political, economic and social networks, local and regional authorities can concurrently bring these two worlds together in formal and informal assemblies and foster dialogue and partnership leading to a coordinated education and training, industrial and employment policy of benefit to the area, the business sector and the individual citizen.

Local partnerships are invaluable, as was pointed out during the workshop that I have attended on fitting actions concerning the integration of young people into the local environment. It is these local and regional partnerships, bringing together social and economic partners, education and training establishments, parents, students, youth associations, etc. which can help provide effective solutions in integrating young people, not only into the labour market, but also into social and civic society. Local and regional authorities across the EU can act as honest brokers in bringing people together and providing a neutral setting for the fullest exchange of views and experiences. We are there — use us! Such partnerships can help ensure that education and training are used as effective regeneration mechanisms promoting the transfer of skills to problem areas and matching skills to local labour market needs and local development strategies.

It is at local and regional level where the majority of innovative and creative approaches are found. Disseminating best practice of these experiences can help ensure that successful innovation projects become part of mainstream policy. It is the COR's view, therefore, that this resource should be more fully tapped and we need to look for ways and means whereby this valuable work can be made available to a much wider audience.

The contribution of education and training in combating social exclusion is now given increased recognition in the proposals for the ESF in the Agenda 2000 dossier on the reform of the Structural Funds. The COR looks forward to commenting on this issue in its future work on the subject and examining in particular the kind of synergies that will exist with the new generation of education, training and youth programmes — a dossier for which I have been appointed Rapporteur of the COR. I look forward to reviewing the report of this conference in that context.

The COR will be hosting a Forum within the framework of its July Plenary Session on Education and Training: the Keys to Employment. The Forum will present examples of decentralised initiatives in the fields of education and training by towns and regions which have contributed towards employment creation. Based on the COR's contribution to the European Employment Summit in Luxembourg and its resolution on territorial employment pacts, the Forum will underscore the COR's commitment to promoting employment, which is a top priority for the EU: a priority which I believe everyone should subscribe to — and not merely in words, but in actions.

In its recent opinion on Towards a Europe of Knowledge, the COR gave much emphasis to the role of education and training in supporting the integration of disadvantaged groups in particular. This is fundamentally linked to the issue of access to training opportunities and in particular access to new technologies which has been the theme of one of today's workshops. We have voiced in many opinions, our concern that disadvantaged groups should not be disenfranchised from new technology and the learning opportunities that can stem from that technology. We must not create a new class of disadvantaged — those who, for whatever reason, do not have ready access both to new technology and the training and education needed to use this equipment and its associated software effectively. We need to think through our provision of teacher training in this regard.

Another important tool in combating social exclusion is intercultural education. The COR has issued an Own-Initiative Opinion on this subject and I had the honour of being a co-rapporteur. This opinion concerns, not only combating racism and xenophobia but also promoting the integration and participation of all citizens, regardless of their ethnic and cultural background in the education and training system. In many Member States there is a tendency for low levels of achievement and high levels of exclusion vis-à-vis ethnic minorities. Intercultural education is a tool which can help tackle this problem.

Exclusion from the educational system is the first step towards marginalisation, followed by exclusion from the employment system and, by extension, from cultural, social and civic life. The contribution of Second Chance Schools in providing opportunities for young people has been welcomed by the COR and the presentations given during this conference indicate how useful this initiative is. However, we must not lose sight of the objective of lifelong learning for all, as stressed in the COR Opinion on the White Paper on education and training, teaching and learning — Towards the learning society.

The COR maintains that steps should be reinforced to provide preventative measures for pupils with special needs as early on as possible and continuing throughout life, following a lifelong learning approach. School failure must be arrested from primary school level and teacher training in this area should be supported, as discussed in another workshop session. As an aside, the COR has stressed the need to update teacher training across the EU. We really need to be radical and ensure that our teachers are indeed trained in modern methods and are equipped both with the skills needed for the 21st century and the flexibility of mind to ensure that these skills are continuously renewed and honed to reflect future — as yet unknown — needs. The COR has stressed the need to ensure that all young unemployed people are able to participate in training schemes and is pleased to note that this figures as a priority recommendation in the Luxembourg Summit on Employment.

Another important area of activity in this field is apprenticeship training which if properly adapted can be a very successful form of training for disadvantaged young people. Here I have in mind something akin to the new modern apprenticeships being pioneered in the UK, rather than some of the medieval practices which used to be the norm even as late as the 1950s and 1960s. The COR has also welcomed the opportunities afforded by the European Voluntary Service in providing an educational tool outside the formal school and vocational training systems to these young people, in particular those who have difficulty in participating in existing EU education and training programmes. I would, however, urge caution to those who think that this would be a cheap method of solving any shortages in the formal school and vocational training systems. Volunteers, however well meaning and enthusiastic, are unlikely to have either the skills or the experience needed to deal with schoolchildren, students or trainees. That is not to say that their offers of assistance should be discarded out of hand, but care should be exercised as well as close supervision and support from those trained to do this particular job.

I would just like to end by saying that I hope that these issues concerning the objective of combating social exclusion through education and training will be given emphasis and support within the framework of the new generation of education, training and youth programmes.

As final remarks, I would like to underline how important it is to have forums such as these to be able to exchange information and good practice in this field. The potential use of the new technology to achieve this proposal is both innovative and exciting. There are dangers which we have been made aware of but I believe that the advantages outweigh the dangers. Therefore we welcome the proposal to establish a network infrastructure to enable this exchange of experiences to continue beyond this conference.

Integrating all young people into society through education and training

Christoforos Korifidis,
Member of the ESC Bureau

Director-General,
Ladies and gentlemen,

In my capacity as representative of the Economic and Social Committee, I would like to begin by thanking Mr O'Dwyer for inviting us to this conference and for giving us the opportunity to express our views on this subject.

However, before I do so and before I outline a specific proposal from the ESC on the problem of exclusion, I think it would be useful to look briefly at a number of other important points of a more general nature, concerning the future of education and the role of the European Commission and of all who work in the field of education — including all of you — in the future.

The following points are the published views of the ESC and thus represent its official position on the subject of education and training.

Point one:

In its opinion on the White Paper on education and training — teaching and learning — towards the learning society the ESC made the following points:

- It described the White Paper as 'being of the greatest importance as a starting point for discussion and examination of problems relating to the current situation in Europe and the outlook for the future'.
- It also said that it 'provides an accurate picture of European economic and social development, as well as of what is needed to bring about a smooth transition from the present situation to the learning society of the future'.
- Finally, it said that 'the aim of achieving a learning society cannot be reached by a Member State pursuing separate paths of strategies, or by summit-level discussion, investigations or choices. The only way to bring this about is a comprehensive and consciously systematic social effort. This social effort must possess a common and acceptable vehicle for coordination, common and acceptable procedures for reconciling opposing views and common, clear and acceptable subordinate objectives. Only the EU and its bodies, particularly the Commission, can coordinate this social effort to bring about a learning society.' We should all remember that the decisions taken today on education and training will determine the way in which Europeans think, their outlook on life and on their fellow men and the values of society 20 years hence. In other words, provided that Europe's citizens are also able to be competitive, these decisions will determine their ability to survive.

Point two:

The ESC feels that it is essential to make key decisions to determine the principles on which the future of education in the European Union will be based:

- Should we aim for selective education or education and training of a high quality for everyone throughout their life? The ESC would opt for the latter.

- Who will pay for education and training and how? The ESC regards education and training as commodities, which a democratic society has a duty to guarantee to all its citizens without exception.
- How much importance should be attached in curricula to humanitarian values, the development of a democratic and social conscience in pupils, the development of tolerance towards and solidarity with our fellow men, especially the less able, and the recognition and acceptance of differences in age, colour, race, sex, religion and ideology, and what should the content of these studies be? The ESC feels that education should cover these issues.

Point three:

The ESC stresses the importance, for the future of the EU as a whole, of the Commission's proposal to set up, gradually, a 'European educational area'. It feels that this proposal:

- fills a crucial gap which the national education systems are clearly not filling;
- contributes — within the framework and terms of the Treaty — to the coordination of the national education systems, making them more effective and competitive in the production of knowledge and also in imparting that knowledge to young people and to citizens in general;
- can, through the system of life-long education and training, give the European citizen the personal, productive and politico-social skills appropriate to the present climate and needs, without being divorced from the roots and values which have shaped European civilisation (centred on the individual, without excluding anyone and allowing for the conscious and effective participation of citizens).

Point four:

The ESC lays particular emphasis on the key importance of improving the quality of basic general education and of ensuring the coordinated exploitation of the national education systems' immense combined strength. It therefore calls on the Commission to exploit all existing ideas and to introduce shrewd measures that will help to eliminate the inflexibility holding back nearly all the national education systems.

Point five:

With regard to the third general aim and problem of exclusion in general, the ESC:

- agrees that a second chance of social integration should be given to young people who have been, or are likely to be, excluded from the education system, and considers the Commission proposal to set up 'second chance schools' to be a 'desirable and acceptable solution';
- it points out that the education system must be flexible so as to also provide a second chance for adults with a low level of education, thereby removing the risk of their being socially excluded on these grounds alone;
- it considers 'second chance' schools to be only a stopgap solution, and points to the importance of strengthening 'first chance' schooling.

Furthermore, the ESC would again stress the risks inherent in the transition to a new world where there will be unlimited access to knowledge, unimaginably fast dissemination of information and completely different conditions and means of communication.

The emergence and growth of new and deeper divisions, both within societies and internationally, between information haves and have-nots is the most likely outcome unless efforts are immediately stepped up to involve, if possible, all Europeans in every aspect of change.

This is also the reason why the ESC places such emphasis on the need for policies to be developed immediately to prevent the marginalisation of large sections of the population, in particular of high risk groups which for various reasons do not have access to new technologies and thus to new knowledge.

These preventive policies include developing the concept of lifelong learning in practice and in its widest possible sense, ensuring that all Europeans have the opportunity to use and benefit from the new information and communication technologies, and, in general, creating an environment in which the learning society can be actively achieved, step by step, by the citizens.

For these major policies to be developed successfully, the ESC feels that there must be coordination between the centre and the regions (EU, Member States and local government), between individuals and society and between the public and private sectors.

It also feels that the Commission and other EU institutions should become the driving force in instituting and completing the processes that will lead to the creation of a learning society in the European Union.

ESC proposal to combat exclusion:

In addition to the above aims and measures, the ESC re-submits its proposal to adopt, promote and generalise the establishment of remedial aid in schools, as a means of fighting exclusion.

The idea is similar to that of the 'accelerated schools' which have grown up in the United States. The aim is to combat the early exclusion of pupils from learning and knowledge. Exclusion of this kind, which is not always total, results from difficulties which many pupils face — usually at a very early age — in integrating into school life. These difficulties arise for different reasons but can usually be eliminated by remedial aid at school. This involves diagnosing the problem and eliminating it by adopting an appropriate teaching method on a partly or wholly individualised basis. It should be provided within the existing education system, within and outside the school timetable and using teachers with the relevant specialisation. It should also apply not just to the weaker pupils but also to those whose performance is outstanding, in advance of their age level, and who will therefore also have difficulties in integrating into school life.

School failure and the social marginalisation of young people who have no qualifications

Dr Ulrich Haase
Federal Minister for Education,
Science, Research and Technology

It is good that this conference is returning to the political dimension of the task of integrating marginalised young people into vocational training and the world of work. I am grateful to have this opportunity of discussing with you Germany's experience. I associate with this three objectives:

1. We must repeatedly review our ideas and measures at national and international meetings. This is an opportunity to do so.
2. We need to step up our exchanges of views, and in particular on the problems faced by every country in Europe in connection with education. We need common fundamental principles for securing a foundation for qualifications in the Member States of the European Union. And we need a social Europe. A completed vocational training course is the admittance ticket to living and working to the full.
3. Lastly, the third objective for me is that we should all understand more clearly what the European Union can and should do in an effort to overcome these problems. I should like to stress that Germany welcomes the inclusion by the Commission of the combating of social marginalisation in its 1995 White Paper as one of its five main objectives. I was interested to learn that the Commission is considering a major conference on this subject during the next year's German Presidency. We will gladly support any such move.

I should now like to return to the matter of our experience. In our efforts to help young people access the labour market we have had some successes but many problems remain.

As successes I would include:

- That according to Eurostat the unemployment rate among young people aged under 25 in Germany has been 10.3 % on average throughout 1997. This is admittedly relatively high but the decisive factor is that the duration of such unemployment averaged only 4.6 months.
- Our system of vocational training schemes, which guarantees a high standard of training. About two-thirds of each year's intake complete what is known as the dual system. There is agreement between the political actors and the social partners to the effect that every young person in this system should have an opportunity to undergo training.
- That, on the basis of this agreement, a comprehensive system for integrating the marginalised has developed since the 1970s. It is organised nationwide via job centres and schools. The job centres placed 199 000 young people in 1997 through various measures relating either to vocational training or preparation for vocational training. To these can be added some 105 000 young people who are attending schools to complete a vocational training preparation year or a basic vocational training year. The job centres spend yearly about DEM 5 thousand million on this work, which also includes expenditure on the rehabilitation of young people with disabilities. Funds from the European Social Fund are also used for this purpose. It is generally agreed in Germany that these funds are being well used. As part of the current action plan on employment the resources available to the job centres for this purpose have been raised by DEM 26 million.

This brings me to the most serious and persistent problems facing us in connection with the integration of young people into the world of work.

- The first problem concerns the provision of training places. Every year in spring a major campaign is mounted to encourage the training sector to offer every young person a place in a training scheme. In 1998 we need about 645 000 places if we are to meet demand. We call this step towards training the first threshold. Efforts on behalf of the marginalised clearly need to be intensified when there is increased competition at the first threshold due to a lack of training places. That is the case today.
- The second problem relates to the level of qualifications required of trainees. In many professions these requirements are extremely high. About 15 % of trainees in Germany currently have the school leaving certificate (*Abitur*). The law allows trainees to enter into training contracts even if they have not completed their schooling but in practice there is evidence that those who leave school poorly qualified have the poorest chances. We want to retain the high standards but we must differentiate and proceed case-by-case in order to avoid writing off the marginalised from the outset. Briefly, the dilemma is that the standards required are being raised and young people are often not able to keep up.
- This leads us to the third problem to which I would like to refer. I will call it the problem of the learning culture. We could ask whether the young people about whom we are talking today are able and keen to learn at all. Many social, psychological and educational factors obstruct their willingness to learn. These factors range from broken families to social dysfunction and frustration at school and may even extend to a complete refusal to learn and dependency on alcohol and other drugs. Any measures adopted to integrate the marginalised must take account of this factor and help the young people to regain the learning culture, a culture of lifelong learning. Youth work, social work and tuition often have to work hand in hand on this.

How can we solve these problems? What relevant experience can we pass on? I shall consider only a few aspects:

- The first and most important aspect is that in Germany the integration of the marginalised has become a permanent system in support of vocational training.
  This integration of the marginalised comprises the basic vocational training year and the vocational training preparatory year, both of which are completed in schools (65 000 participants). In addition there are many auxiliary schemes provided by the job centres ranging from demonstration courses to one-year basic training courses and special integration aids with extra courses on offer to restore linguistic and training skills with special courses being available for people with disabilities.
  Experience has shown that these aids are a necessary part of today's training and qualification systems. It is not just a case of crisis management but of something which is indispensable in a society which sets ever greater store by knowledge and which at the same time must be very keen to ensure that everyone is given a chance so that social cohesion is not lost. Ladies and gentlemen, we will in future have no choice but to keep on providing this assistance.
- The second experience that I should like to relate is that the success of such assistance is determined largely by the extent to which account is taken of the particular requirements of a young person who is poorly placed in society and faced with learning difficulties. It is this experience which prompted the Council at the time to state in its opinion of 6 May 1996 on the Commission's White Paper that the problems of failure at school cannot be solved by a single institutionalised measure. The experience can therefore be described thus: only flexible, individual, local and versatile solutions can provide effective assistance.
- However, the above presupposes that a third major experience is possible; namely, that in the long term such assistance can only be provided by reliable cooperation between many partners at local level. Vocational counselling provided by job centres cooperating closely with schools is a key issue in this respect. The schools, chambers, undertakings, local authorities and of course the political players at State and federal level must work together. This also applies to the authorities responsible for administering the European Social Fund, which is so important for the new German states. Experience shows that alliances have to be formed for auxiliary measures of this type. Based on consensus, individual and flexible solutions can be found where they are needed.

The integration of the marginalised involves a European dimension not without reason. Even if the local level is the most important aspect of all the possible solutions, the European Union is nevertheless an extremely important player in efforts to integrate young people on the labour market successfully. Let me quote from the joint position on European vocational training policy adopted by the Federal and *Länder* Ministers in Germany on 17 June 1996:

'The European Union must step up its efforts to reduce the number of young people without vocational qualifications and to establish this objective as one of the principal components of a social, labour market and training policy geared to complementarity. Successful measures in this field must be incorporated into national policy to a greater extent. Top priority must be given to providing support for young people and helping them to integrate.'

Let me remind you that the transition from school to working was the subject of many successful Community-level measures during the 1970s and 1980s. Not unrelated to this is the fact that the Treaty of Maastricht (Article 127) mentions expressly the objective of Community activities being to 'facilitate access to vocational training'.

What can the European Union do to facilitate access to vocational training? The Union must help to develop the wealth of experience within Member States in this difficult field. It can use pilot projects to prompt new solutions and use the resources of the European Social Fund at many locations to provide effective help. Clearly, the Union cannot relieve the Member States of the burden of securing a future for all young people. But it can ensure transparency, issue challenges and call to mind. The new procedure for establishing action plans for employment and evaluating them at European level demonstrates clearly the scope available.

These reports bear out what I have said here today and which I can now summarise:

- Integrating the socially marginalised is an essential and constant task if existing qualification potential is to be fully mobilised and social cohesion secured. Policy on general vocational training carries a heavy burden of responsibility.
- The solutions must be targeted, adequate, flexible and varied. There are no patent solutions.
- In view of the problems faced by many young people it is of central importance that a responsible community be established comprising all levels of personnel working in the field. This community must invest heavily in political terms every year to ensure that new ideas are put into practice.

Part II

Combating failure at school: Prevention and remedial strategies

The studies summarised below were funded by the Socrates programme of the European Commission, DG XXII

Dropping out and secondary education

Massimiano Bucchi
IARD Research Institute (I)

IARD, a research institute in Milan, has just concluded the first year of a two-year transnational research on 'Dropping out and secondary education'. The study is carried out in 18 European countries (i.e. the 15 EU countries, Liechtenstein, Norway and Iceland) and is supported by DG XXII in the framework of Socrates programme.

In the European Union a relevant percentage of young people drops out of national secondary education (universities excluded) without having obtained even the lowest qualification legally recognised by each system of education.

In particular it is possible to identify drop-outs as:

1. Those who do not continue their education after obtaining the school leaving certificate and do not enrol on a vocational training course.
2. Those who stop attending during or at the end of their first year after enrolling on a secondary education course.
3. Those who fail to obtain the certificate awarded at the end of a secondary education or vocational training course.

The main scope of the study 'Dropping out and secondary education' is to provide detailed national reports in order to evaluate the number and distribution of drop-outs by type of school, gender and geographical area and to make a comparative analysis of drop-out profiles and their relationship with pre-existing structures of inequality.

This analysis will allow defining and implementing preventive actions toward those categories most exposed to this phenomenon, both at a national and at a European level.

On this basis, the first goal of the study is to provide evidence of the state of the art of current information in the educational field with specific regard to the possibility of analysing the phenomenon of differential selectivity.

The sources examined were the official national statistics and all those available, provided they were systematic, organic and continuous in order to draw up a detailed picture of numbers, the social and geographic distribution and degree of involvement in the educational processes.

Secondly, the study intends to identify any possibility of constructing relevant markers of selectivity, taking into account the validity in different territorial locations and their capacity for detecting social differences.

The study has been divided into three sections:

1. Description of national school systems.
2. Nature and state of statistical sources on high-school education.
3. Definition of the markers that can be extracted.

The extraction of suitable markers will allow investigating the relationship between the educational system and the global social system in order to measure:

1. The transmission of knowledge and basic social skills.
2. The link between education and economy.
3. The existence of equal opportunities (access to education, use of resources and results obtained).
4. The availability of services to satisfy the demand for education and the ability of the system to respond to the needs and expectations of individuals.
5. The link between education and quality of life and the contribution of education to the satisfaction of material needs.

According to this general framework, three types of markers have been identified:

1. Markers of involvement in the school system.
2. Markers of process in educational involvement and exposure to the school system.
3. Markers of probability of school leaving.

The study highlighted the variety of situations characterising the different countries involved, first of all in producing information regarding school selection and drop-outs. This is due to three factors:

- The different dimensions and the social/institutional diversity of the countries considered are *per se* conditions that may generate a greater or smaller incidence of the phenomenon. In the smallest countries having a stronger cultural and social uniformity, the phenomenon of dropping out is not relevant.
- The variety in the organisation of the several official bodies and agencies producing statistics implies a different methodological approach and rigour and/or higher/lower attention to issues as dropping out, which are often deemed marginal compared to economic matters. Therefore, not in all countries is there an updated and articulated production of statistics in the field of education.
- The incidence itself of the phenomenon and the connected social impact may stimulate in different ways commitment on the part of official bodies to survey, analyse and discuss it.

Overview of the results

In order to present in a synoptic form the situation of education and dropping out in the various countries involved, four comparative tables have been structured referring to aspects relevant for understanding the phenomenon considered:

1. The first simple scheme has been constructed to show in a compact form and in a comparative perspective the key elements of the national education systems (Table 1).
2. The second scheme represents an attempt to show innovation in legislation during the past 10 years, with the assumption that this information demonstrates the close attention that is being given to education (Table 2).
3. The third table is dedicated to the ways in which official statistics on education are drawn up (Table 3).
4. The last table shows the most meaningful markers of the dropping-out phenomenon resulting from a simple elaboration of official information (Table 4).

Some elements must be underlined for better understanding the proposed schemes:

- There is no comparable body of sources available for immediate and simple consultations.
- The statistical information differs from country to country in terms of production and publication time.
- In some cases it was difficult to reconstruct the processes by which these statistics were produced.
- Only a few countries officially run special surveys relevant for the study.
- The situation of the various countries has been sometimes simplified in favour of a more symmetrical and comparative overview.

Table 1 allows proposing some interesting considerations:

- The various countries have opted for a different school starting age in a fairly direct ratio both to the preceding education delegated to other agents and to the degree to which these pre-school systems are made use of.

- The duration of compulsory education is quite variable (eight years in Italy, 12 years in the Netherlands, Belgium and Germany).
- Those countries that have made fewer innovations in terms of general organisations require the first choice of an educational route to be made at a younger age.
- There is a greater degree of homogeneity (a range of two years) in the normal age of access to university, which may, however, be preceded by a wide variety of routes, either in educational or vocational training.

Four categories of legislation can be identified, according to Table 2:

- The countries that have been subject to centralised regimes for long periods have felt an urgent need to set up new general legislation to re-define contents and organisation of the school inspired by criteria better suited to ongoing phases of social, economic and technological growth.
- The countries that traditionally dedicate closer attention to education (France and Spain) have taken specific actions relating both to the organisation of school systems and to the connection with the labour market (vocational guidance, career counselling, link with enterprises, etc.).
- The countries in which legislation is extremely dated (Italy, Germany and Austria) but where exist a 'grey area' of legislation, which is delegated to bodies at the outer limits of the State apparatus and partly intended to modify individual aspects of school system.
- It seems that there has been a considerable return to legislative action in the past five years as education is perceived as an area of strong social concern on which each country's potential development depends.

The dropping-out phenomenon

In some countries there is still a disproportion of educational opportunity according to gender and geographical location, in others the whole of the female population is recuperated by the school system, to the extent that it prevails both in terms of involvement in the system and in terms of regularity; in the same way, geographical location seems to be a key factor mainly in terms of proximity to large or medium-sized urban centres, with less importance noticed in terms of location in less favourite areas (although there are still countries, such as Italy, in which there are considerable differences in involvement from north to south).

Clearly the social conditions of the family are still decisive everywhere in providing opportunities for continuing with education or dropping out early and limiting opportunities to routes closely linked to employment.

In some countries, however, there is a powerful emergence of phenomena, which are a novelty for European tradition: the limited educational opportunities for recent emigrant groups seem to be the new phenomenon characterising education. It requires action based on an original approach, respecting the groups' cultures of origin, and the establishment of processes of integration that are completely innovative, with close attention to the issues of ill-being and deviant behaviour in social life.

We therefore have an indirect measurement of the phenomenon of dropping out, which does not take into account either the stage at which it occurs, nor the consequences or the social profile of the individuals affected.

It provides us a general indication of the number of subjects involved and is, therefore, the basis for the construction of exploratory schemes and for models of interpretation, which link it to other phenomena, characteristics or social situations.

As is clear from the analysis of available data, in some countries the phenomenon of dropping out markedly coincides with the end of compulsory education. This is for instance the case of Portugal (from 16.9 % young people not attending school at the age of 15 to 16 — still within the compulsory segment — to 40.4 % youngsters not attending school at the age of 17 to 19), Great Britain (from 27.1 % to 40.8 % passing from 16 to 17 years of age) and the Netherlands (the number of youngsters not attending school within the 17 years age cohort more than doubles in the passage to the 18 years age cohort — from 9.4 % to 20.2 %). In other countries, instead, other factors must add to the simple effect of leaving the compulsory segment. In Italy, for instance, the rate of drop-outs continues to grow even after the 'big leap' towards post-compulsory education, steadily increasing with the age cohorts (from 12.1 % at the age of 15 to 19.6 % at 16, involving at the end of the segment more than one third of the young people). In Iceland a similar pattern is also observed, where the rate of non-attending youngsters actually doubles with the exit from compulsory schooling but after that rises up to 36 %. In Greece this problem seems to reach its peak among the 18 countries considered: while the rate of non-attending subjects is still slightly more than one fifth of the overall population (22.4 %) at the age of 16 (i.e. right after the end of the compulsory cycle which lasts until the age of 15), it continues to rise together with the increase in age jumping to 80.6 % for the 18 age cohort. At that same age more than 80 % of youngsters are still at school in Germany, Norway, Sweden and Finland. In Greece and in Italy other factors combine with the structure of the school system in producing such large proportions of drop-outs: the major factor seems to be territorial differences. While in Italy the sharp dichotomy is that of north/south, however, more subtle articulation and diversity with regard to geographical areas seem to be observable in Greece.

Another remarkable factor, albeit more or less common to all countries, seems to be that of gender: males being more affected by the phenomenon of dropping out than females of the same age.

The collected material allows highlighting some aspects of the national statistical documentation officially and currently produced:

1. EC's institutions play a relevant role in suggesting and imposing rules tendentially common to all countries and standardised, for drawing up of statistical data. The definition of concepts, operational processes for collecting data, attempts to set down the information collected in comparative tables seem to have reached a fair degree of uniformity. All this despite the fact that their starting points are very different in terms of nature of organisation, the aims, the ways in which the various routes are differentiated.
2. Notwithstanding this tendency at uniformity, there still remain marked differences, either in the procedure for drawing up data or in its specifications and arrangement. These differences directly affect the possibility to obtain compact and meaningful markers of the performance of education systems.
3. The usual current statistics are more and more frequently integrated with surveys that are new both in their design and their aims and which enable the schooling processes and routes of the younger generations to be better examined. The use of longitudinal surveys is becoming widespread: these studies are conducted directly on the individual concerned and are rich in surrounding information not directly relating to schools. The results are very significant but difficult to generalise as they refer to a specific generation under examination and they depend on the precision with which they are carried out. The interference of specific structural conditions, the risk of losing information because of the mobility over the territory, the importance of keeping a parallel check on the general evolution of the country considered, the importance that individual changes in the family may assume, the costs in terms of efforts and money that are involved in longitudinal surveys are all factors that make this type of study extremely precious and difficult to repeat.

The first year of IARD research has yielded the following insights:

(a) It is difficult to access information as statistics are too general, mostly without in-depth information on local and social differences concerning the subjects involved in dropping out.
(b) Homogeneous data and formats are lacking, especially due to the diversity in school systems and in the surveying/data presentation methods.
(c) Basic information is hardly ever followed up, particularly with regard to the construction of indicators that make it possible to summarise the actual nature and incidence of dropping out.

This initial research has enabled IARD to identify the availability of specific studies, carried out on a national and regional scale by universities and research institutes, which may be carefully analysed and used to integrate official data. Work carried out during the first year of the project has served to put together a statistical overview of dropping out:

- existing official documentation was examined;
- quantitative aspects and cumulative data were considered;
- and markers produced in each country in order to focus on those more easily comparable were identified.

The main results produced so far can be summarised as follows:

- there is diversity in the degree of attention paid to this phenomenon in the different countries. It mainly depends on the size and intensity of dropping out in each educational system;
- basic statistics and markers produced by official bodies differ from country to country and are only partly governed by the general definitions promoted by European institutions. Other definitions seem to be tailored to specific national needs and situations;
- education reforms in the last 15 years have varied greatly from country to country, but they have all attempted to decentralise organisation, moving decision-making powers to a sub-national administrative level and granting individual scholastic institutions greater autonomy and responsibility. This process has been accompanied by the transfer of coordination and the setting of functional norms to the national level.

Table 1: Schematic view of European school systems

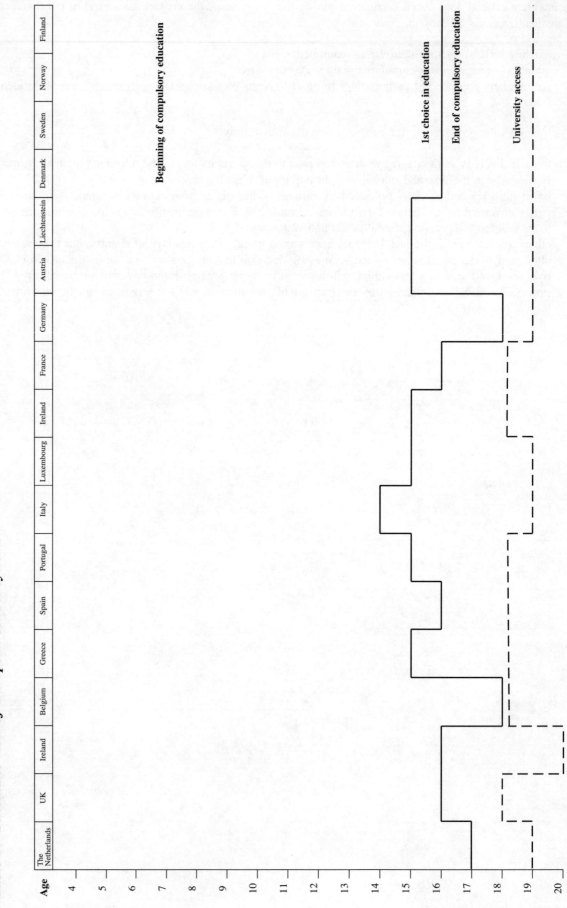

Table 2: Legislative innovations

Year	The Netherlands	UK	Iceland	Belgium	Greece	Spain	Portugal	Italy	Luxembourg	Ireland	France	Germany	Austria	Denmark	Sweden	Norway	Finland
1996	LIP																
1995			LGen													LGen	
1994										LGen				LGen			
1993											LIP						
1992		LIP			LIP		LIP										LCic
1991						LGen											
1990															LCic		
1989							LCic		LCic		LO LCic			LIP			
1988																	
1987							LGen										
1986						LGen		LCic									
1985																	
1984																	
1983				LGen													
......																	
......																	
1979								LCic									
......																	
1972												LGen					
......																	
1962													LGen				

LGen: Legislation of a general nature
LIP: Legislation relating to professional training
LCic: Legislation relating to the first or/and second educational cycle
LO: Legislation relating to career counselling

39

Table 3: Official sources on school attendance and dropping out

	Greece	Spain	Portugal	Finland	UK
Institution	Ministry of Education and Religion	Ministry of Education and Culture	Ministry of Education	Ministry of Education	Department of Education (England, Wales, Scotland, Northern Ireland)
Office	Statistic Service	Planning and Statistics Office	Department of Programming and Financial Management		
Frequency	Annual	Annual	Annual		Annual
Dimension	Census survey	Census survey			Panel study
Unit of analysis	School	School	School		Individuals
Tool	Questionnaire	Questionnaire	Optical reading form		Postal survey
Target group	(a) Students (b) School (c) Teaching staff (d) Administrative staff	(a) Students (b) Drop-outs (c) Foreign pupils (d) Teaching staff (e) School (f) Not teaching staff (g) Not teaching services	(a) Students (b) Outputs (c) Teaching staff (d) Schools		(a) Students (b) Teaching staff (c) Schools (d) Finance (e) Qualification (d) Destination
Main features	(a) Sex, age, other socioeconomic features (b) Sex, age, training (c) Functions (d) Premises, rooms etc.	(a) Sex, age, redoublement (b) Sex, schooling level (c) Sex	(a) Sex, age		
Main publication (last issue available)	'Educational Statistics'	'Statistics on Education' (1994/95)	'Statistics on Education' (1993/94)	'Education in Finland' (1994)	
Survey					'Youth Cohort Study' began in 1984/85 (England and Wales) and Scottish School Leavers Survey (since 1984); Statistical bulletins on school leavers for Northern Ireland.

Continued on next page

	Ireland	Austria	Norway	Sweden	Italy
Institution	Department of Education and of Enterprise and Employment	Federal Ministry of Education and Culture in cooperation with . the Austrian Statistical Office	Statistics Norway	Statistics Sweden	Statistic National Institute (ISTAT)
Office					Department of Education
Frequency	Annual	Annual	Every autumn	Every autumn	Annual
Dimension	National stratified random sample of school leavers interviewed one year after leaving school				Census survey
Unit of analysis	Individuals	Pupils			School
Tool	Interviews				Questionnaire
Target group	(a) School leavers	Students	(a) Students enrolled each autumn in secondary school	(a) Students enrolled each autumn in secondary school	(a) School (b) Students
Main features		(a) Sex (b) Age	(a) Sex, age, residence, citizenship and place of birth (b) line of study	(a) Sex, age, residence, citizenship and place of birth (b) line of study	(a) Sex (b) Redoublement (c) Examination results
Main publication (last issue available)	'The Economic status of school leavers' (1993-95)	Osterreichische Schulstatistik	'Statistical Yearbook of Norway'	'Statistical Yearbook of Sweden'	'Statistics on Education'
Survey	'Annual School Leavers' Survey'	Schulabbruch, Schulwechsel und moglichkeiten der verbesserung im informationssystem	'Statistics Across Borders' and a special publication 'Ukens Statistikk (Weekly Bulletin of Statistics)'	'Statistics Across Borders' and a special publication 'Utbildningsstatistisk arsbok' (published every year)	

Continued on next page

	France	Germany	The Netherlands	Iceland	Luxembourg
Institution	Ministry of National Education	Federal Government and the Region (*Länder*); for vocational education the Federal Ministry for Education, Science, Research and Technology	Central Bureau of Statistics (CBS)	Statistics Iceland (Hagstofa Islands)	Ministry of Education, Department of SCRIPT
Office	Office of Evaluation and Forecasting	Statistical Office			STATEC (Central service for statistics and economic studies)
Frequency	Annual: at the beginning of each school year	Annual	Annual	Annual	Survey at periodic intervals
Dimension					
Unit of analysis				Students	Pupils and Teachers
Tool				All full time students	
Target group	Pupils in first and secondary education				
Main features	The evaluations consider 10 academic disciplines and three non-cognitive domains: (a) school life (b) methods of working (c) public-spiritedness			Information on each individual's type of studies	
Main publication (last issue available)	Annual publication: School geography, Statistical References on School Education, School Situation.	'Statistisches Bundesamt' (1995 or 1996); "Statistische Landesamter' (1995); 'Berufsbildungsbericht' annual report of vocational training (1995); Mikrozensus: a representative survey on social mobility (1991).	'The Statistical Yearbook', 'The pocket book of educational statistics', 'Statistics of general secondary education', 'Statistics of pre-vocational education' and 'Transferral within the educational system and entrance into society'.	Statistical Yearbook of Iceland and Statistics Across Borders	
Survey	Periodical publications: (a) Evaluation: Gazette of the European Network of Persons in charge of School System' evaluation policies (b) Education and Training (c) Notes of information: brief on the latest surveys or studies (weekly) (d) Education and information files. Each file gives a very detailed account of one dimension of the school system (around about 15 files per year)				

Table 4: Dropping out rates (^{1})

Age	Greece	Spain	Portugal	Finland	UK	Ireland	Norway	Sweden	Italy
15	14.9	6.4	15.0			4.3			12.1
16	22.4	19.4	26.0	4.0	13.0	8.9	5.0	4.0	19.6
17	37.0	17.0	33.0	8.0	26.0	18.1	9.6	5.0	28.0
18	80.6	39.0	45.0	18.4			16.5	17.0	32.4

Age	France	Germany	The Netherlands	Iceland	Luxembourg	Denmark	Austria	Belgium
15	2.0	1.3	1.1		n.d.	3.0	5.0	
16	4.0	2.8	2.5	11.0	n.d.	7.0	8.0	
17	8.0	6.4	9.4	23.0	n.d.	19.0	14.0	
18	16.0	15.6	20.2	35.0	n.d.	30.0	39.0	13.2

(^{1}) Year of reference is different in each country and varies from 1993/94 to 1995/96.

Fostering educational success of socially excluded youngsters: from prevention to remedy

Dr Ides Nicaise
HIVA
Catholic University of Leuven (B)

Three types of strategies

The literature on educational inequality suggests a basic distinction between obstacles on the demand side of education (which can be referred to as 'unequal opportunities' depending on the socioeconomic environment of the pupil) and on the supply side ('unequal treatment' or 'discrimination' on the part of educational institutions).

The former group of factors are related to the socioeconomic handicaps of pupils from poor families: material or cultural deprivation, poor health, unstable family relationships, lack of social and cultural capital, etc. (i.e. factors which are more or less 'exogenous' to the education system). The latter group have to do with the education system itself, or more precisely, the way in which educational institutions and their agents (teachers, counsellors, school principals, etc.) prejudice pupils from lower social backgrounds.

The distinction does not imply that education policy has no impact whatsoever on the environmental circumstances: for example, financial incentives within education can help overcome the material obstacles to a successful school career, although obviously the education system is not responsible for them. Rather, the distinction helps in classifying strategies to promote educational equality. Thus we will consider two types of strategies: those aimed at ensuring *more equal opportunities* (or *more equal access*), and those aimed at *more equal treatment* within education itself.

Besides being 'demand-focused', equal opportunities strategies will also typically be multidimensional and multidisciplinary in nature. Given the multiple causes of unequal opportunities (financial, physical, cultural, social, emotional, etc.), only multi-faceted responses will effectively combat this source of educational disadvantage.

'Equal treatment strategies' on the other hand focus on the elimination of discriminatory behaviour within the education process at school. They are thus typically 'supply-centred', i.e. concentrate on what happens within the school or classroom. A great emphasis will be put on the role of communication, because the lack of communication between the school and the home environment of pupils proves to be a major source of prejudices and discrimination.

Over the years the emphasis has shifted back and forth between both types of strategies, not infrequently accompanied by ideological debates on the causes (structural or otherwise) of educational inequality (Silver and Silver, 1991; Connell, 1994).

In our view, controversies of this type are of little use, since both types of cause have structural roots: in one case outside the education system, and in the other case within it. Moreover, both types of mechanism interact with each other. In the light of this, it would be naive to tackle the problems using one-sided strategies.

A third, somewhat hybrid approach can be added to the list: strategies for *more equal outcomes*. The latter are based on the conviction that equal treatment in itself will not be sufficient to restore the balance in favour of young people from the most disadvantaged backgrounds: rather than 'non-discrimination', they imply 'positive discrimination'. Part of the calling of education is after all to help *reduce* social inequalities, not to reproduce them as neutrally as possible. Educational priority policies (consisting mainly of extra funding for schools with a concentration of disadvantaged students) are a standard example of this approach.

Equal outcomes strategies in fact combine elements of both previous types of strategy. However, unlike equal opportunity strategies, they are focused on *outcomes* rather than *access*. In this sense, they can also be characterised as 'ex-post', remedying strategies. For example, targeted pre-school programmes and second-chance schools are two types of compensatory programme. However, pre-school programmes can be regarded as a typical equal opportunity approach because they contribute to a more equal start in primary school; whereas second-chance provisions aim at equalising outcomes.

Contrary to the equal treatment approach, equal outcomes strategies discriminate positively in favour of disadvantaged groups. Hence, they are also more targeted on the specific needs of minorities than equal treatment strategies.

After reviewing examples from the six countries represented in our research network, we end up with the following checklist of strategies.

Equal opportunity strategies

1. *(Extension of) statutory education*: As far as the spontaneous demand for further education falls short, public authorities have tried to impose a minimum participation on every individual. The minimum school-leaving age has been raised in nearly all EU countries over the past 15 years. On the other hand, in some countries the law guarantees each young person a set of (extra) educational services as a counterpart of these minimum requirements (as we shall see, for example, with the Scottish Education Act and the Spanish Social Guarantee Programme).
    The enforcement of compulsory education is not without difficulties: premature dropout and truancy have become serious problems. Hence, several governments have launched special measures to register and monitor school attendance, to encourage pupils and parents to comply with the measures, and to prevent dropout. Examples are the 'Well-prepared Start' programme in the Netherlands and the 'Education for All' programme in Portugal. Of course, dropout prevention is a more or less explicit objective of many other types of intervention, such as alternative curricula or integrated services to pupils and families, which will be dealt with in other sections.
2. National governments have introduced a wide range of *financial assistance measures for low-income families*: grants, loans, means-tested educational provision (tuition fees, transportation, meals, clothing, book grants, etc.), special measures relating to family allowances, tax credits (as far as they are related to education and to disadvantaged groups).
3. Equal opportunities are also promoted through the provision of a wide range of *integrated services* (psychological, social, cultural, medical, material, etc.) for disadvantaged pupils, often organised and delivered at local level. These services aim at improving the general conditions for effective participation in education, mostly in close collaboration with parents and other actors in the neighbourhood. Some nice illustrations are found in the Flemish primary schools that were sponsored for some time by the King Baldwin Foundation.
4. One of the most effective strategies in promoting equal opportunities has been the development of *pre-school stimulation programmes* for disadvantaged groups ([1]). The Irish 'Early Start' (and its preceding local experiments — the Rutland Street and Kilkenny projects) are undoubtedly the most outstanding examples of this kind in Europe. However, other interesting lessons can be drawn from the 'travelling pre-schools' in isolated rural areas in Spain and from various local projects with babies and toddlers in other countries.

---

[1] General pre-school provision (such as daycare centres, nurseries or infant schools) will not be analysed in our study, unless they include special services for socially excluded children.

Equal treatment strategies

1. In order to combat selectiveness, socially biased failure, streaming and creaming mechanisms, there is a great need for *curricular reforms* in the sense of comprehensivisation, more relevant learning contents for everyday life, and less discriminating certification strategies. The recent major reforms in Portugal (1989) and Spain (1990) went a long way in that direction.
2. Note the distinction between reforms of the *general* curriculum (covering all students and thus improving equality) on the one hand, and the development of flexible, alternative curricula for pupils with special needs on the other. At this point we will deal only with the former type of curricular reforms, as the latter actually implies a different treatment of disadvantaged groups with a view to equalise educational outcomes. Flexible, alternative curricula will therefore be discussed in the context of 'equal outcomes strategies'.
3. Besides curricular reforms, it is worthwhile to study the (potential) impact of some alternative pedagogical approaches (Freire, Freinet, Feuerstein and others) on the educational success of disadvantaged children. Experiments in Belgium and Spain suggest that such approaches may be of particular interest for these children; paradoxically, however, their access to such schools is problematic because of institutional and financial barriers.
4. Discriminatory behaviour is often due to social prejudices resulting from the ignorance of teachers (and indeed, of the entire school staff) with regard to social exclusion. *Teacher training* can play an important role in helping teachers recognise and understand processes and victims of social exclusion, and to respond adequately.
5. Combating discrimination calls for more intensive *communication between schools/teachers on the one hand, and parents/local communities on the other*. Some interesting experiments have been carried out recently, ranging from home-school-community liaison in Ireland and a School-Environment Link project in Portugal, to parents' groups and sensibilisation campaigns among pupils in Belgium.

Equal outcomes strategies

1. A first type of issues in this respect consists of *categorical measures*, i.e. specific services being offered to groups with special needs with a view to a better integration: intercultural education for ethnic minorities, special services to traveller children (well developed in Portugal, Ireland and Scotland), integrated education for disabled children (Belgium, the Netherlands, Spain), travelling schools and networks between schools in isolated rural areas (Portugal, Spain).
2. As disadvantaged groups need greater investments to attain a given outcome, most Member States in the EU have now adopted one kind or another of *educational priority policies*: i.e. extra funds for schools faced with a concentration of children at risk. Educational priority funding has 'territorial' and 'categorical' variants; in some countries both variants co-exist (the Netherlands).
3. Positive discrimination in favour of marginalised groups can take the form of *differentiation, i.e. extra pedagogical support within schools or classes* (remedial teaching, differentiation within the classroom, learning support to pupils, teacher counsellors, etc.).
4. Finally, a range of *alternative curricula* has been developed in order to ensure a maximum of access to recognised (if possible, standard) qualifications for socially disadvantaged students, mostly at upper secondary level: alternating forms of vocational education combined with work experience, apprenticeship systems, and remedial programmes or lower-level certificates for students who fail in mainstream programmes.
5. The demarcation line between flexibilisation (aiming at equal outcomes) and streaming (a form of social discrimination) is sometimes a very thin one. 'Flexible curricula' should ideally lead to standard (mainstream) certificates. The integration of specific 'sidetrack' certificates into the national qualification structure is a rather second-best solution, which cannot really be regarded as an 'equal outcomes' strategy. Empirical evaluations are needed in this context, more than anywhere else.

Examples at micro-level

Equal opportunity strategies: the Pilton Early Intervention Programme (Edinburgh, Scotland)

Lothian Region Education and the City of Edinburgh Council Committees made funding available for a three year period (1994 to 1997) with the intention of improving children's attainment in literacy in their primary school years P1 to P3. Four primary schools participated in the project from areas described by Edinburgh District Council as '... in terms of multiple deprivation, the worst hit areas. On indicators of unemployment, long-term unemployment, large families, single-parent families, free school meals, housing benefit and housing conditions these areas came off worst'. The funding provided was used to employ two home-link teachers, 1.6 FTE (full-time equivalent) learning support teachers and six nursery nurses (appointed to the four project primary schools).

Working on the assumption that remedial action later in a child's schooling is not as effective as early intervention, the project was intended to establish an integrated and coherent programme of early intervention for children from pre-school to primary 3.

To achieve these aims the *nursery nurses* appointed by the project were to assist teachers with literacy instruction. At nursery level the project aimed to improve pupils' knowledge about books, letters, rhyme and phonology. Each nursery involved in the project was provided with a package of relevant books and other materials to assist this process.

Home-school link teachers were given the task of supporting parents in their role as educators of their own children. This involved holding workshops for parents on early literacy in both pre-school and early primary years, the development of resources to enable parents to stimulate literacy and the provision of opportunities for children and parents to work together.

In the early years classes of primary 1 to primary 3 (P1-P3) *classroom assistants* were employed to assist teachers in literacy instruction and generally to increase the amount of time that each child spent reading.

P2 and P3 teachers were asked to build upon this programme and to supplement it with an emphasis on word patterns, reading by analogy, specific methods of spelling instruction and punctuation.

There was a marked improvement in the number of children with a good alphabetic knowledge at primary 1 level. The proportion of pupils with the ability of automatic recognition of almost all letters (necessary to read effectively) increased dramatically from 22.7 % in 1994 to 72.5 % in 1997. Reading attainment has also increased from 10 % of pupils reading ten or more words correctly in the Burt Vernon Test [2] in 1994, to 40 % in 1997.

Further improvement was also achieved at Primary 3 level, a measure of which is the fact that the percentage of pupils spelling at above average levels has increased from 9.5 to 33.5 %.

The overall success of this pilot scheme was instrumental in the Scottish Office decision to fund a nationwide early intervention programme.

Equal treatment strategies: De Buurt (Gent, Belgium)

'De Buurt' is a small school (<100 pupils) in a popular district of Gent, with a concentration of immigrants and disadvantaged groups of native Belgians. The school was set up within a local network including (at different stages) a community action group, a children's club, a 'neighbourhood café', literacy courses for adults, evening classes for children, and an integration centre for migrants. The school gradually became an independent body, although it maintains close links with other initiatives and with the inhabitants in the neighbourhood. It deliberately opts for a small scale, with children from the neighbourhood receiving priority in enrolments. The school population is fairly mixed, but includes a strong minority of migrant children (1/4) and a number of children from socially excluded homes.

The school propagates an emancipatory vision of education, and explicitly aims at minimising educational inequality. The responsible team labels its educational approach 'experience-based project work', in which (even more than with Freinet schools) pupils' problem-solving capacities are actively stimulated.

---

[2] The Burt Vernon Word Recognition Test — is a measure of the number of words read correctly.

Pupils determine (directly or indirectly) the problems they want to elaborate on. As projects exceed the separation between subjects, traditional textbooks have been replaced with worksheets developed by the school team. 'Project periods' (usually weeks) are alternated with 'exercise weeks'.

You will see no 'classes', no 'teachers', but 'living groups' (2-3 years; 4-5 years; 6-8 years and 9-11 years) and 'companions'. The system of living groups prevents individual children from always being the eldest or the youngest, the most or the least able pupil, etc.; it also avoids grade repetition to some extent. Each living group is accompanied by two 'companions', which also implies teamwork, differentiation and prevents an exclusive dependence on a single teacher.

Parents' partnership is a cornerstone of the school's strategy. The 'heart' of the school is a large kitchen where parents can have coffee when they bring their children to school in the morning; it is also the room where joint meetings are held monthly with parents and companions, by living group. Some parents are actively involved in the educational and other activities, which creates extra opportunities for differentiation. Others help with material work, but also with supervision, administration and the development of the school's strategy. Even in-service training of the companions is organised in mixed groups with parents. Parents who do not spontaneously participate in such meetings are being visited at home, or in separate group meetings. The school pretends to offer something in return to parents: they acquire new skills like assertiveness, expression, organisation, democratic participation, citizenship. From the early 1970s on, 'De Buurt' pioneered in *educational community action* as a pilot project subsidised by the Department of Culture.

Equal outcomes strategies: achieving success for all in disadvantaged schools (Roubaix and Lille, France)

This is rather a personal experience of an individual school teacher and principal (Mr G. Quinto) in two different schools, 'Littre' in Roubaix and 'Rollin' in Lille.

Both schools are situated in disadvantaged districts and have a mixed population of French and foreign pupils; both were run-down and characterised by violence and high rates of school failure. Mr Quinto's strategy is centred on achieving success for all children. It builds on parents' involvement, citizenship of pupils and proving to the outside world that disadvantaged children are able to learn and even to achieve great things.

He promoted *parents' involvement* by receiving parents personally at the school gate, by home visits, and by mobilising parents for the renovation of the school and the opening of a school library. In one of the schools, a special room was installed for parents. Representation of all nationalities in the parents' committee has been used as a device to foster a maximum of representativeness, etc. for minorities: reports of the committee are being translated into Chinese, Arabic and Portuguese. Some 82 to 88 % of the parents participated in the last elections for the committee.

Mr Quinto tackled violence, not by more authoritarian rules and severe sanctions, but by developing a sense of *citizenship* among pupils. After studying the rights of children, the children themselves – together with the school team — adapted the school regulations. Human rights were also studied, for example, through street theatre on the occasion of the 200th anniversary of the French Revolution, and through sensitisation about the link between poverty and human rights and the history of poverty on October 17 (world day for the fight against poverty). The right to education for all received particular attention — it resulted in new projects within the school, also beyond the school hours: peer tutoring between pupils, reading corner, music corner, excursions, etc.

Besides parents and pupils, the two schools are very committed to liaising with the local and wider community. A piece of fallow land was transformed by the pupils into a playground and a *'resto du coeur'* ('heart's restaurant') for birds: this project was presented on TV. A festival was organised for a well-known poet and singer, Julos Beaucarne (children sang his songs, translated his poems and played theatre for him). The school won a basket-ball competition and the pupils were received at the City Hall. All sorts of cultural activities were organised beyond the school hours, etc. The positive image created through these public events contributed greatly to the reduction of violence and a greater sense of community.

Remedial ([3]) strategies for failure at school in the European Union: An overview and three case studies ([4])

François-Marie Gérard
Bureau d'Ingénierie en Éducation et en Formation (BIEF) (B)

Introduction

Our report is based largely on the findings of a study entitled 'Completing one's education' conducted under the European Socrates programme.

This study was justified by the large percentage of young people in most European countries who leave the education system before they have mastered the whole of the curriculum considered to be the minimum basis for qualification. The deficiencies of these 'school drop-outs' ([5]) are likely to have a major impact on their social and working life and on their personal development. The problem is therefore one of helping these young people to continue to learn and to return to education.

The main aim of this project was to pinpoint, from data available in the 15 EU Member States and the three EFTA countries, what kinds of action seem to offer the most promising solutions to this complex problem and to find out what remediation strategies are applied once young people have failed at school.

It is difficult to provide an overall picture as the many initiatives currently being run are shaped to a large extent by their specific context. 'Dropping out' is defined in different ways that are shaped by the structure of each country's education system. At first glance, the simplest way of defining our target group would be to talk about young people who leave school before they have obtained a qualifying certificate. This definition does not, however, cover every situation. In the northern countries, for instance, almost all young people obtain the upper secondary leaving certificate, mostly in the general stream. Young people who fail to continue their education are therefore considered to be 'young people without qualifications' — even if they possess the certificate — as this certificate does not enable them to find work in the labour market. Norway offers an interesting case in this respect as every young person leaving school obtains a certificate. Depending on the circumstances in which they left school, this certificate will be complete or incomplete.

Many other examples could be marshalled to show that any attempt to draw common threads from fundamentally different situations is well-nigh impossible. We feel, however, that a number of aspects are common to all these specific contexts. We are not talking here about universal truths, but rather overall proposals that should have meaning and should be applicable in different contexts.

The strategies surveyed

The survey studied 153 initiatives in 17 countries. It should be noted that all these measures were retroactive, i.e. they were taking place outside of compulsory education in order to try to find an answer to failure at school.

([3]) The term used in Belgium to define the notion of young people's social and occupational re-integration, term used in France.
([4]) Report prepared in cooperation with Donatienne Colson (BIEF), Claudel Guitard and Natacha Martynow (Experimental education department of Liège University).
([5]) Editor's note: this term covers young people who leave school early, who are expelled or who choose to drop out themselves.

The many initiatives being run for young people without qualifications, their differing objectives and resources, the lack of comparability of contexts, target groups and partnerships, etc., made it difficult but necessary for us to find some way of organising the mass of data that we had gathered.

In order to impose a structure on this mass of information, we took *goals*, i.e. the objectives that initiatives are intended to achieve, as our starting point. Every initiative gives priority to and is characterised by one or more specific goals. These goals shape the form of the initiative and the remediation strategies that it uses. These goals are not exclusive with the result that an initiative may have several goals and be pursuing several strategies at the same time, although in the following presentation each initiative is attached, for reasons of simplicity, to a single goal.

For young people with no qualifications, the six goals that we pinpointed constitute a *path towards integration* — both theoretical and linear — as the following diagram shows.

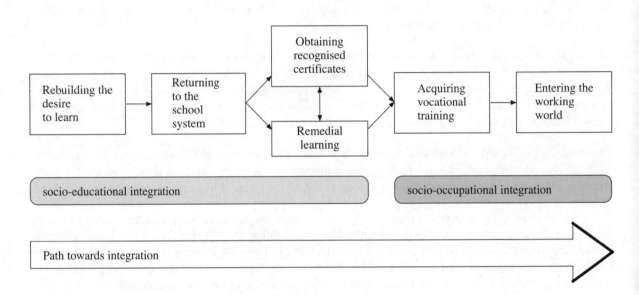

Rebuilding the desire of school drop-outs to learn and helping them to regain confidence in their ability to learn is obviously the starting point of their path towards integration. After this they can return to the education system, re-enter ordinary schools and continue their education in a non-marginal way. The second chance school projects currently being run in 11 countries, with the support of the European Commission, pursue this objective since they attempt to combat exclusion through education and training. The next step — taking a continuous approach — should be for them to obtain certificates and official validation of the (new) knowledge that they have acquired. An integration pathway of this type should ultimately lead to the acquisition of supplementary skills from vocational training so that the young people in question can finally enter the labour market.

We should be careful, however, not to read these categories in too linear a way. Bearing in mind that the theoretical linear path described above is not necessarily followed in practice, it needs to be read in a systemic way if we are to understand the various inter-relationships that exist between these various goals.

Rebuilding the desire to learn

This first strategy comes into play when the aim of the initiative is to help young people to regain self-confidence, to draw up a personal plan, to improve their relationships, etc., or possibly to 'learn to learn' or to provide young people with the resources that they need to continue their education by themselves.

Nine initiatives were explicitly pursuing this goal, in particular including:

- the German Training Assistance Measures (*Ausbildungsbeleitende Hilfen — abH*);
- the Irish Community Training Workshops (CTWs);
- the Norwegian Labour Institute (*Arbeidsinstituttet*);
- the Luxembourg Vocational Induction and Training Courses (*Cours d'initiation et de formation professionnelle*);
- Velorep, in Austria.

While any generalisation would be incorrect, these initiatives seem to share a number of characteristics:

- the initiative focuses on young people in order to increase their *autonomy*, make the most of the *knowledge that they have already acquired* and build on their *psycho-social skills;*
- course timetables and organisation are flexible and give priority to *assisted self-instruction;*
- the stress is placed on helping young people to draw up *occupational and personal plans;*
- a great deal of psychological work takes place with the young people in an attempt to *make the fact that they have failed at and dropped out of school into less of a drama, to increase their self-confidence,* etc.;
- working groups are relatively small and *individual guidance* is often offered.

Returning to school

This second strategy includes initiatives that help young people to return to formal schooling.

We found 52 initiatives of this type, in particular including:

- the German Basic Vocational Training Courses (*Grundausbildungslehrgänge*);
- Young People's Individual Education in Denmark (*Fri Ungdomsuddannelse — FUU*);
- the Dutch Regional Training Centres (*Regionale Opleidingen Centra — ROC*);
- the French Information and Guidance Sessions (*Session d'Information et d'Orientation — SIO*);
- Second Chance Education in Flemish-speaking Belgium (*Tweedekans Onderwijs*);
- the Spanish Workshop Schools and Trade Centres (*Escuelas taller y Casas de oficios*).

These initiatives share the following features:

- particular attention is paid to the *methods that can be used to motivate young people* and to help them imagine their future;
- the *key players in the initiative are the young people themselves*. Time is allocated for drawing up and implementing the personal plans around which their integration pathways are structured;
- young people can take *sabbatical leave* enabling them to take stock, if they need to, as in working life.

Obtaining officially recognised certificates

We found 54 measures intended to help young people to acquire officially recognised certificates. They included:

- the Greek Public Evening Schools (*Δημόσια Εσπερινά Σχολεία*);
- Spanish Adult Secondary Education (*Enseñanza secundaria para adultos*);
- the Finnish Alternative Vocational School (*Vaihtœhtoinen ammattikoulu*);
- the Swedish Individual Programmes (*Det individuella programmet*);
- Portuguese Pre-learning and Learning Schemes (*A Pré-Aprendizagem e a Aprendizagem*);
- Youth Training in the United Kingdom.

Initiatives of this type all had the following aspects in common:

- *self-instruction* tailored to people's experience, needs and interests makes young people the key players in their training;

- the payment of *unemployment and training benefits* for young people in training, *childminding schemes, bonuses* on obtaining certificates, etc., are all aspects motivating young people to attend training;
- *personal programmes,* formulated in line with young people's aspirations, make it possible to help them *to change their behaviour or to adapt to society* (regular responsibilities, problem-solving, independence, relations with family members, etc.). This type of training may help young people to *break away from dependence* (alcohol, drugs) or to see themselves in a different way by helping them to construct *their own professional identity.*

Remedial learning

This category covers initiatives targeted on literacy, the acquisition of basic skills in mathematics and/or languages, general culture, civic education, etc.

Fifty-one initiatives of this type were surveyed, including:

- the Icelandic Municipal Evening School (*Namsflokkar Reykjavikur*);
- the Irish Travellers' Training Workshops;
- Training for Work (TfW) in the United Kingdom;
- the Belgian Work Training Enterprises (*Entreprises de Formation par le Travail — EFT*);
- the Finnish Youth Workshop (*Nuorten työpajatoiminta*).

These initiatives share the following characteristics:

- this remedial learning is accompanied by *support, counselling and guidance* through which *demand can be analysed* and curricula drawn up on a *case-by-case* basis within a *holistic approach* to the individual that is intended to develop his or her *autonomy;*
- part-time work, work *intended to increase occupational efficiency* and the possibility of receiving a *wage*, together with vocational training linked to the job, helps to motivate young people and increases their chances of re-integration;
- substantial *tutoring* and *mentoring* is provided, as well as *assistance* in locating periods of vocational experience or jobs;
- initiatives are based on *partnerships* between official agencies, those involved and enterprises.

Acquiring vocational training

Sixty-five initiatives aimed to teach a trade and included:

- the Luxembourg Anti-Unemployment Scheme (*l'Action anti-chômage*);
- the Italian Employment/Training Contract (*Contratto Formazione Lavoro*);
- the Danish International Youth Cafés (*International Ungdomscafé*);
- the Belgian Employment-Training Agreement (*la Convention emploi-formation*);
- French Local Initiative Additional Training (*la Formation complémentaire d'initiative locale — FCIL*).

The following aspects can be pinpointed:

- the young people targeted by this type of initiative are generally *jobseekers*;
- *enterprise* is a key partner;
- particular emphasis is placed on *occupational integration*;
- *alternance training* makes it possible for young people to *experience work* and to *learn a trade*;
- learning and employment *conditions* are often viewed *favourably* by these young people because they have little to do with the institutional type of education that they have often rejected;
- most of these initiatives do not lead to formal certificates. In some cases *certificates recognised by particular industries* are awarded;
- *individual reviews* and *guidance* and *follow-up* schemes in some cases form part of the pathway and are intended to help these young people to find work.

Entering the working world

Lastly, 72 programmes geared towards obtaining a job were surveyed and included:

- the French Network of Information Facilities (*le Réseau des structures d'accueil*);
- the Austrian Springboard (*Sprungbrett*);
- the Finnish Summer Work Campaigns (*Kesätyökampanjat*);
- Socially Useful Works in Italy (*Lavori socialmente utili*);
- the Luxembourg Labour Market Integration Programmes (*les Programmes d'intégration au marché du travail*).

This final type of initiative has the following features:

- training in a formal context is not the only answer to the problems of young people who have no qualifications. *Individual help* in formulating and following up a plan or th*e possibility of working*, even for short periods, are other ways in which socio-occupational integration can be promoted;
- these schemes often have a positive effect in the long term as they help young people to return, under supervision, to a working environment, to *find out about their abilities* and ultimately to *find a more permanent job*;
- the *partnerships* on which most of these schemes are based are important as they make it possible to take a multiple approach to the young people in question;
- *employers* can use these schemes as a way of meeting one-off needs in a relatively inexpensive way;
- *work experience periods* are often too *short* in relative terms and do not enable young people really to 'prove' themselves, especially as they may be allocated to '*menial and unimportant tasks*' which do not necessarily lead in the long term to a job.

Three case studies

We shall now examine three actual initiatives ranging from the small to the large. These initiatives are working towards all the goals that form part of the path towards integration discussed above.

Velorep: **A social enterprise for bicycle repair (Austria)**

Velorep is a bicycle repair enterprise within the social economy, supported by Salzburg's Job Promotion and Placement Service. Making the most of one of the town's main features — the impressive number of people who travel by bicycle — *Velorep* tries to help young people to learn the basics of life in society through work.

Velorep's aims are to help young people, over a year, to become socially integrated, and to provide them with vocational training and work. They are placed in an employment situation, with a recruitment contract and all the constraints linked to social and working life (punctuality, accuracy, reliability, taking responsibility, respect of others and their work, actual presence, respect of deadlines, quality of work produced, positive contacts with customers, productivity, etc.). When they leave, young people can enter the labour market or attend training.

These objectives are achieved in the following ways:

- occupational aspects:
  - basic training in metal-working
  - the possibility of learning and practising the trade of welder's mate;
- personal aspects:
  - training in perseverance and conflict management
  - increased self-confidence.

53

Velorep has had two strands since 1997: a social-economy enterprise and a workshop in which courses in welding, metal-working, etc., are given to close on 15 young people aged between 18 and 25, all without qualifications, under the supervision of five trainers.

- **A social economy enterprise** (*Sozio-ökonomischer Betrieb*, SÖB)

In the enterprise, young people are employed on bicycle repairs or metal-working (welding). Employment in the enterprise is perceived as the goal towards which all newcomers to *Velorep* should work. This paid work, under a recruitment contract, requires specific skills, experience and a number of qualities such as speed, punctuality and careful work. These skills are developed during the first strand of *Velorep* (the courses).

- **A training department** (*Kurs-maßnahmen*)

In this department, trainees are younger (between 15 and 18) and have not as yet had any training in or experience of *Velorep*'s work. Nor do they have the maturity needed to hold down a job. The technical training that they attend takes place largely in a working environment that mirrors real life as closely as possible. Priority is given to instruction in basic social skills (punctuality, accuracy, team-working, etc.).

Newcomers to *Velorep* are not placed directly in the social enterprise. They attend courses and, depending on their abilities, their desire to learn and their achievements, they then move on to the SÖB workshop. They are generally motivated to move on to the enterprise, especially since wages are higher and their status changes (workers rather than trainees).

Young people attending *Velorep* do not have to register with a school. In some cases, they decide by themselves to register for evening classes while at *Velorep*. They can attend the courses run by the *Berufsförderungsinstitut* (BFI) which is an agency of the Federal *Länder*. In Salzburg, the BFI runs courses providing vocational education for young people (*Berufs-vorbereitungstraining für Jugendliche*) [6]. *Velorep* receives a special subsidy if its young people attend BFI evening classes in order to pay for their education.

Velorep seems to be helping the young people involved who all say that they are pleased to be part of the initiative. *Velorep* does not, however, offer training recognised by an official certificate. Young people are also reluctant to tell potential employers that they have been working at *Velorep* as they are often categorised as 'disadvantaged young people'. Employers prefer to recruit young people who have followed recognised apprenticeship schemes.

By way of conclusion, the concept of the social-economy enterprise seems to be a good way of reaching the target group of young people without qualifications and may prove to be a positive strategy in remedying failure at school:

- the enterprise is both social and economic: it focuses on individuals, but places them in an economic environment;
- young people are brought face-to-face with the realities of production work: analysing customers' requirements, respecting deadlines, accurate work, whether this work meets the customer's expectations, etc.;
- the continued existence of the enterprise depends on the young people who are responsible, through their work, for bringing capital into the enterprise;
- both job and basic skills are learnt through work;
- the enterprise is part of a local context and has to keep in touch with changes in its surrounding environment. This makes it possible for the young people to be integrated in a broader system and to take part, albeit indirectly, in local life — where this is possible;
- the young people's status changes from 'unemployed' to 'employed' making it possible for them to experience, albeit in a protected environment, direct contact with the working world. This change in status helps them to acquire greater self-confidence and respect for themselves and their work;
- the work that they carry out is not just routine: it is carried out for a specific customer and employees are responsible for all the stages of this work right up to completion; they are able to feel proud of what they have achieved;

---

[6] For more information on BFI courses, see Colson D., Gerard F.-M., Guitard C. & Martynow N. (1997, March), 'Continuing One's Education' project, Austrian national report, *Bureau d'Ingénierie en Éducation et en Formation* (BIEF).

- the division into two departments, one being in some ways a kind of antechamber for the other, helps young people tangibly to measure their progress (change of status, doubling of pay, etc.). The flexibility of this formula and the fact that it is very much in keeping with the ways in which young people learn, could well be copied;
- the socio-educational approach that is used with the young people means that they can be viewed as whole people. They are considered as full partners and can work towards skills that are broader than those connected with the job alone. They are therefore free to become involved in their work and in training that develops at their own pace;
- through their work, young people who have in most cases experienced failure and disillusionment can learn to overcome their past experiences and regain a positive image of their future.

Barcelona Workshop Schools *(Escuellas taller de Barcelona)* — Spain

The Barcelona workshop schools is one of the initiatives that Spain has introduced to try to find answers to the problems of young jobseekers aged between 16 and 25 who have never worked, have no vocational qualifications, are looking for a manual job and are excluded from society and employment. These disadvantaged young people often have dramatic personal and socio-occupational histories. They are perceived as social and educational outcasts. They also reject the basic principles of these two systems.

The training is intended to provide these young people with an opportunity to acquire basic and vocational abilities and skills while helping them to gain confidence in themselves and in their abilities and making them responsible for their own lives. Particular attention is paid to the individual development of these learner-workers.

The training strategy is based on alternance between theory and practice. The young people attend training, whose philosophy is one of *learning by working*, where they learn the techniques of a trade as well as basic knowledge and job-finding techniques (information on the labour market, job-finding strategies, improved management skills, creation of one's job, etc.). Trainees also learn to *work while learning* a trade through the hands-on experience that they acquire by working on a real socially useful site, in this case the renovation of the historical heritage of the city of Barcelona. Learner-workers therefore carry out tangible work whose results they can see and appreciate. This provides them with work experience that they can talk about when looking for a job. It also helps them to build up confidence in themselves and in their abilities.

The strategy is based on teacher-learner group work (one teacher for 8 to 15 learners); the aim in classes is to generate an active and participative dynamic and to place the stress on developing creative attitudes and personal autonomy while leaving aside abstract knowledge not connected with reality. Learner-worker groups of different 'ability' are often advocated since this enables exchanges and interactions between the strongest and the weakest.

There are two training modules which are generally run in the workshop school which is located on site:

1. an induction training module, lasting six months, given over to vocational training and generally taking place in the workshop school;
2. a module alternating training with work, under a contract of employment between the learner-worker and the promoter (*Barcelona Activa*) for the remainder of the heritage rehabilitation project.

An 'integration' module is one of the key aspects of this training. The aim is to provide these learner-workers with the resources that they need confidently to enter the labour market. The key areas that are tackled with these learners are self-esteem, methods and guidance. This module helps to monitor the young people from a personal and professional point of view.

Young people's personal and professional advancement is a key concern from the point of view of sustainable social and occupational integration: acquisition of working habits (cleanliness, respect of working hours, clothing, etc.), greater personal autonomy, making the most of oneself, self-esteem, discovery of one's own abilities, etc.

Learner-workers also receive pay for the work that they carry out, which is a motivating element.

At the end of this training, follow-up is provided by *Barcelona Activa:* contacts with enterprises for the occupational integration of the young people; contacts with the young people to find out whether they are working and whether they are working in the trade that they have learnt.

Different kinds of people are involved in the scheme. Trainers are experts in their trade. They are engaged on a half-time basis which enables them to continue with their jobs and therefore to keep in touch with labour market needs and technical developments and to be better teachers.

Other people generally have university or higher degrees in education or psychology and have skills in group dynamics and adult training. They are involved at various stages of the project. Expert trainers and school directors receive special training.

Barcelona Activa's action has had concrete effects:

- 50 to 60 % of the young people trained in Barcelona's workshop schools have found work — of some kind — in the months following their training;
- they have had actual experience of work;
- the rehabilitation of the city is a key aspect of the project and is of considerable social utility while at the same time meeting the local market demand;
- finding work for the unemployed helps to stimulate economic life;
- the young people become more mature: some young people arrive 'knowing nothing' and make considerable progress from the point of view of their professional skills and maturity;
- the older trainees are rapidly motivated, learn more quickly and make clearer choices even though their self-esteem is often very low when they arrive;
- they become aware that work is something serious and develop a sense of responsibility with the result that they have more of a will to work;
- they feel that they are more sociable, can work as a team and are less introverted.

The learning method provides these learner-workers with two points of reference: work and training. They become aware themselves that they need theoretical knowledge if they are to work more efficiently with the result that they gradually become more interested in training.

Regional Training Centres — Netherlands *(Regionale Opleidingen Centra (ROC))*

As a reaction to the high percentage (30 %) of young people leaving school without qualifications, regional and national measures have been introduced ([7]) in the Netherlands to prevent young people who are considered to be at risk from dropping out of school permanently and to help those who leave school without certificates to complete their courses.

Following the establishment in 1996 of the WEB (*Wet Educatie Beroepsonderwijs*), the *Regionale Opleidingen Centra* (ROC), or Regional Training Centres, were set up. These centres provide a regional framework for separate and different facilities. Goals are specific to regions. The aim is to shift everything to do with vocational training and adult education to the same place. The ROC target is to help 10 to 15 % of people lacking basic qualifications over the next five to ten years.

The *Regionaal Opleidingen Centrum Oostelijk Zuid-Limburg*, for instance, has some 10 000 students and 650 staff, mainly teachers. It has four units:

- an education and advice centre (*Advies-en Studiecentrum*) which represents adult education;
- an economic college (*Economish College*) which is responsible for finance and for managing teachers;

([7]) For further information, please see: BIEF, Socrates 'Continuing One's Education', Netherlands national report, February 1997.

- the *Middelbaar Dienstverlenend Gezondheidszorg Onderwijs*, in the health care field;
- the *Technisch College Heerlen*.

Young people can follow two study routes:

- the *Beroepsopleidende leerweg*, i.e. the former vocational secondary education scheme for adults. This includes a minimum of 20 % practice and a maximum of 80 % theory;
- the *Beroepsbegeleidende leerweg*, i.e. the former apprenticeship system which includes at least 80 % of practical experience and a maximum of 20 % of theory.

There are four training levels:

- educational assistance (*assistent opleiding*), i.e. guidance and transitional programmes lasting six months to one year which are intended to help trainees to choose a training scheme and to make progress in medium or long-term courses;
- basic vocational training (*basisberoeps opleiding*): short courses, spread over two to three years, teach the basic abilities needed to carry on a trade and pave the way for entry into longer courses;
- vocational training (*vak opleiding*) made up of intermediate courses providing the skills needed for self-employment. These courses last from two to four years.
- intermediate management training (three or four years) and specialist training (one or two years) (*middenkader opleiding*).

Courses are run in four different sectors:

- technical work and technology;
- social services and health care;
- finance and administration;
- agriculture.

Students have to choose the training that they wish to attend, the level that they wish to achieve and the method that best suits them (20–80 % or 80–20 %).

A Guidance Centre (*Trajectbureau*) has recently been set up (1997). This centre works with the other institutions and in particular with the agencies that deal with young people who are failing at school or who lack qualifications. Young people are referred by the *Regionaal Meld en Coördinatiepunt*, by local authorities, by special education schools, by schools, by the employment office, etc. The centre also works with other partners such as the *Jeugdwerk Garantie Wet* and the CBB (Jobseekers' Training Centre).

The *Trajectbureau*'s role is to find out whether these young people can be placed in the regional training centre system. If they cannot be placed, there are two possible solutions:

- the young person can attend a training course, but has to attend a pre-training course (given by the ROC) beforehand;
- workers call on their social network to send the young person to the most appropriate facility (for instance a drug rehabilitation centre).

It therefore has three main tasks.

Orientation and guidance

Given the wide range of courses available, one of the centre's tasks is to guide students. Guidance and orientation sessions are held, particularly for students considered to be at risk.

Operation

The centre acts as a mediator between teachers and students. One of its tasks is to find solutions for everyone's problems, at both individual and group level. Teachers can request assistance in the same way as students. Teachers can therefore ask for help with methods, discipline problems in class, specific difficulties with students or with the organisation of classes or lessons. The aim is one of cooperation and of channelling everyone's energies into working together and developing a common policy. The *Trajectbureau* is gradually trying to step up its work with teachers and to reduce its work with students. According to those involved, working with teachers helps indirectly to reach a much larger number of students and at the same time to reduce similar work with students.

Training in basic skills

The centre's third role is to run training courses that provide basic skills. Lessons, pre-training courses, etc., are run for students considered to be at risk, i.e. likely to drop out. Lessons are given in basic skills such as Dutch and social skills (learning to communicate with teachers and colleagues at the school, and with colleagues and employers). The Goldstein method is used. Around 100 students considered to be at risk attend this pre-training.

By way of conclusion, combining different institutions within the same facility may be a useful way of combating the problem of failure at school:

- given the range of methods used and the range of training modules, students can readily move from one to another. If someone is experiencing difficulties in one type of study, a new direction can be found for them;
- detecting people who are 'at risk' makes it possible to offer appropriate resources to those who need them;
- pre-training schemes are organised to reduce the risk of failure;
- students can be more readily monitored during their courses at the centre;
- through its network of contacts with partners (RMC, JWG), the Department of Education is able, via the ROCs, to locate where people are failing at school. Accurately identifying this target group is one of the main problems that the government faces;
- the organisers of the ROCs are aware that they cannot find answers to all the problems experienced by some young people. In some cases, these people have such problems that it is impossible to place them in the institution even when they have attended the pre-training run by the *Trajectbureau*. The organisers are therefore envisaging the creation of a special facility that should help them to resolve this problem.

Part III

Thematic workshops

First session
7 May 1998
Exchanges of experience and identification of good practices

Second session
8 May 1998
European network cooperation methods

Workshop 1

What teaching methods for the integration of young people in difficulty?
(Individualisation of pathways, active teaching methods, consideration
of the achievement of experiences, counselling and guidance, etc.)

Vejle kommunale Ungdomsskole in DHI
The integrated programme for people threatened with lifelong marginalisation

Eva Søndergaard,
Coordinator DHI
Communal Complementary School (DK)

I am a coordinator of one of the leading Vejle kommunale Ungdomsskole projects. We are members of the Second Chance School project network in Denmark and the Second Chance School is due to open in June.

DHI (integrated programme for people threatened with lifelong marginalisation) in Denmark

The project is supported by the Danish Government and Social Affairs Ministry and there are links with the Labour Ministry and the Education Ministry. The project started in 1996 and will continue till 1999. Two project leaders are employed and they have a 'monitoring group' (experts from the labour market, development centres and a former Social Affairs minister) to advise and counsel them.

There are six projects from various regions in Denmark linked to the DHI. All of them work with young people who for various reasons have dropped out from the education system and society. The projects are very different: job centre, production schools, printing press, youth school and a pottery. All projects are aim to provide young people with the opportunity to develop individual skills and widen their prospects. For this purpose a realistic scheme has been implemented, all the projects are also setting up support and contact facilities.

Vejle kommunale Ungdomsskole (unit 1), where I work, is a youth school run by the local authorities. We work with young people between 14 and 18 years of age. One project has ages up to 24. There are different projects:

Communal Youth School

1200 students. These come from the normal school system and attend evening classes to improve their knowledge of languages, maths, creativity, etc. There is a club where students can arrange parties and excursions, etc.

The 'Youth' City Council

Comprised of selected young people between 15-24 years, who will be responsible for the city's youth policy.

Projects aimed at young people who lack standard education and employment

Aktiv Skolen

15 pupils between 13-17 years who for various reasons never completed the normal education system.

They take the same exams in Danish and maths as they would in the 'Folkeskole'.

10th Class

For young people who wish to study in the morning and work in the afternoon.

They take the same exams in Danish and maths as they would in the 'Folkeskole'.

DHI (integrated programme)

This is linked to PAU, the Bridge Building Class and the FUU (Open Youth Education).

PAU (practical standard education)

A three-year project for impaired learners. It has 24 students and provides practical training, learning through doing, employment training in the work place, courses at AMU (training for the labour market). At the end of the course they are placed in a flexible employment scheme in which the government pays 50 % and the employer 50 %. The rate may be modified to 40/60 or 80/20 according to how well the individual is able to work.

This course is individually tailored.

We have rented a house and begun a college, three students are presently in the accommodation. It provides assistance to students who need extra attention on leaving home. After a year, they move into a small young people's apartment, but remain in contact with the trainer in the college who provides help when it is required.

Bridge building class

A three-year project for young refugees.

There are 8 trainees in a beginner's class, 12 students in a bridge building class and 4 students in a project which aims to provide them with stability.

Practical training includes courses at other schools (technical schools), training in the work place, as well as courses in Danish, maths and a great deal of counselling and guidance which is carried out in close co-operation with the parents.

Pupils from the bridge building class may later proceed through the normal education system, open youth education, in-company training or employment.

In Denmark 75 % continue in education after basic school, 25 % either do not continue or receive a basic education. Therefore, the government decided that this group should have the possibility of drawing up their own course of education, the aim being that each young person gets a personal training schedule guided by an advisor. It is akin to building with Lego bricks: first a training period in a work place, a period at a technical school, a VUC or perhaps a high school. Through this education the young people obtain personal and social skills and vocational qualifications which may form the basis for further education or for employment.

Open youth education (FUU), bridge building and common labour education (EGU) are three new offers from the Danish Ministry of Education and have now been in existence for two years.

They are very popular, with 7 000 pupils in open youth education, 2 500 pupils in common labour education. This education is offered to all young people who for some reason or another could not follow the usual educational system. The integrated programme mainly deals with the mass of the pupils. What will they need in order to gain such an education? How to provide support and contact arrangements for these young people? Our experience shows that if we succeed in building a solid network of local authorities, the labour market and the educational system, and link them to a teacher trainer, work colleague or tutor whom the pupil feels confident with, we will provide the best conditions.

Socrates basic skills project (ODL)

David Horsburgh
Lewisham College (UK)

Introduction

This project is funded by the European Socrates Open and Distance Learning programme. The project is led by Lewisham College but has partners in Portugal, Austria and Finland. They are:

• INETI Instituto Nacional de Endenharia e Tecnologia Industrial — Portugal;

• Karkku College of Home Economics and Social Services — Finland;

• Volkshochschule Florisdorf — Austria.

It arose from some work done at Lewisham College within a Resource Based Learning project. This explored the use of the New Reading Disk which was produced by Cambridge Training and Development and the Basic Skills Agency. The resource was used by young learners to develop basic literacy skills. During the project it was discovered that the CD-ROM needed to be accompanied with high quality learning materials that could help structure the activities of the student.

The Socrates project is developing this original work. A review of multimedia-based materials aimed at developing literacy skills is being undertaken in all the participating countries. It is intended that guidelines should be developed for the production of learning materials to accompany selected CD-ROM based multimedia resources. We are also interested in finding out the best ways in which teachers can use such resources to achieve successful learning experiences for their students. At the end of the first year of the project it is intended to test multimedia resources and associated paper-based materials with learners in a variety of contexts.

Target groups

The students with whom we are particularly interested in using these resources with, frequently have problems with basic reading, writing and communication. These problems will often be a barrier to employment and can serve to exclude individuals from many normal day-to-day activities. In Lewisham College we are particularly interested in working with the 16 to 19 year age group who have special educational needs and older students on pre-employment programmes. In our partners in Portugal and Austria there are interests in adult literacy development. In Finland most of the students fall into the 16 to 19 category.

Why multimedia?

Multimedia has been seen as a particularly useful learning resource for inclusive education since it is:

• flexible — allows the learner to use it at times that are convenient;
• self paced — allows the learner to progress at a speed that is appropriate to him/her;
• interactivity — allows students to be more active in their learning and receive feedback from the medium;

- non-linear — allows for consideration of a wide range of information in an order that can be selected by the students rather than imposed by a learning regime.

The participants of our project are well aware of these benefits. However there are still many individuals who are directly involved with the facilitation of learning who remain to be convinced.

Review of resources

There is not a large range of multimedia products on the market that is particularly suitable for developing basic skills literacy. This is especially true in Finland, Austria and Portugal. Much of what is available is very unsophisticated in its application and allows limited freedom and interactivity for the student. The best examples identified so far are the New Reading disk from Cambridge Training and Development and Words in Action from IBM.

These products are not widely available at the moment in languages other than English. There is a need to explore if they could be adapted to meet the needs of other EU countries. The project is actively engaged in this process at present. In Finland due to the lack of basic skills multimedia available, the project team has concentrated on the use of vocational and general CD-ROM titles such as an encyclopaedia and natural history resource to develop basic skills. Learning materials have then been produced that develop general literacy and writing skills.

Evaluation methodologies

An initial evaluation framework has been established for basic skills multimedia products by Lewisham College. This will be reviewed, adapted and validated in our second transnational meeting in July. We wish to take particular account of transnational considerations relating to evaluation. Different national academic and learning traditions may make different demands on a multimedia resource. It is intended to identify core evaluation procedures for all countries, however these will need to link with the specific needs of each tradition.

Selection of resources

The following resources have been identified for further study:

- Words In Action made by IBM in the UK.
- New Reading Disk made by CTAD in the UK.
- *Einblicke Miteinander,* produced by the Goethe Institut in Munich.

A variety of vocational and general CD-ROM titles in Finland, e.g. Facta an encyclopaedia and a home economics CD on baking.

Learners' needs

An examination of the needs of both learners and the facilitators of learning is now well established within all the partners. These needs will be carefully considered in the production of learning materials to accompany our chosen resources.

Teachers' needs

The process of using multimedia in learning poses new management challenges for the educator. It must be decided whether the resource is to be used in traditional whole-class sessions or through open learning.

There needs to be a clear understanding of how such a resource can be integrated into other learning methods that are being employed. As other work has suggested, it is important to establish the nature of the dynamic between learner, software and educator. In this project we must also consider the role of associated learning materials in this process.

Teachers are used to using books, assignments and other paper-based materials in their work. They have grown up with such media and more importantly have learnt how to use it. This is not the case for multimedia, as a result there is a lot of fear and resistance among teachers. This can partly be dispelled by well-supported 'hands on' experience which introduces teachers to technical as well as pedagogical support issues. However, no matter how good support and training is, there comes a time when educators must take the 'leap of faith' and start to use multimedia within learning programs. The project will examine strategies to achieve this aim particularly in the second year.

Structuring of the pedagogic process

It is felt that in order for multimedia to be used purposefully, it is necessary to structure the learning experience for the learner. In the project this is to be done by the development of paper-based materials that can be used alongside the software. These resources will introduce the learners to the resource and help them to navigate their way through it. In addition a number of exercises/tasks will be developed which are linked to clear learning objectives. There will be opportunities for students to assess themselves and also relate to teachers/facilitators to get feedback on their progress.

Development of ODL learning materials

Initial findings suggest that the design of learning materials for students with literacy learning needs must be given great thought. Good materials avoid a number of common design faults. The project team in the UK has spent much time on the design of such learning materials. Their findings will be presented at our next project meeting in July. Initial thoughts are listed below in a checklist of good characteristics of paper-based materials.

1. Do they provide an advanced organiser (some text that prepares students for the activities that will follow) within the resource so that students have an understanding of the structure and purpose of the materials?
2. Do they clearly 'signpost' the students through the materials so they know where they are going and what they should be doing?
3. Do they explain the software interface where necessary if it is not clear?
4. Do they keep the language level appropriate to the audience?
5. Do they avoid long, over-complex sentences?
6. Do they avoid small point sizes for text and fonts that can be distracting?
7. Do they have a common feel and approach?
8. Do they use signs, symbols, key words and graphics consistently?
9. Do they use plenty of white space between text to enhance readability?
10. Do they use graphics only where they assist understanding in the learning process?
11. Do they use consolidation exercises to ensure students understand how to use the resource?
12. Do they provide a sense of achievement for the learner through self-assessment exercises?
13. Do they add additional exercises which complement activities on the CD-ROM and test understanding of subject matter?
14. Do they ensure all activities fit into the original advanced organiser?
15. Do they try to cater for a range of learning styles?
16. Are they aimed at a particular audience/group of learners?

Initial findings

From the work that has been done so far a number of findings have been noted. In the second year there will be a detailed investigation of initial outcomes to see if they are accurate across the project. These include the following points:

- The evaluation of multimedia must include the views of students. Younger students especially often have high levels of IT skills. They are able to provide fast feedback regarding the quality of a resource in motivational terms.
- Teachers need to develop technical as well as pedagogical skills so they are able to feel confident in the use of CD-ROMs in the learning environment. This has been possible through group-based action research activities within this project particularly in Finland.
- Clear instructions and teachers' notes must be available or produced to ensure the resource can be installed, used and integrated into learning activities. Where installation is difficult technical support is essential. In Portugal the project has concentrated on how teachers can be trained to use CD-ROM multimedia resources with potential learners in the area of basic skills.
- The importance of the ODL approach cannot be underestimated in rural areas. Students often live long distances away from educational institutions, therefore the opportunity to work independently and effectively at a distance is greatly valued.
- Translations of CD-ROM must support not only the language but the culture of a country. Whereas in Austria they are to be used with second language learners the resource must be flexible enough to support more than one culture.

Learning is an individual process

What has been confirmed by work in this project is that learning is essentially an individual process. Aiming a multimedia resource at particular groups is a problem since all groups are made up of different individuals with differing needs and learning styles. The development of basic skills is often a particularly individually focused process. Many of the students who have problems with basic skills have failed to learn them by conventional teaching methods during their educational careers. Multimedia can be regarded as a tool that will require different approaches to be taken to learning and can be used by skilful teachers to address particular learning needs. This, however, is essentially a student-centred process, therefore it is important not to underestimate the new skills required by teachers and facilitators of learning in terms of planning, preparation and monitoring of learning mediated through multimedia.

Preventing exclusion at college level

Eeva Laurila
Helsinki Roihuvuori Vocational College

The Helsinki Roihuvuori Vocational College was founded in 1904. It is the second oldest vocational college in Finland with approximately 800 students. There are three main study areas, these are Hotel, Restaurant and Catering, the Food Industry and the Textiles and Clothing Sector. The college is located in the east of Helsinki, where there are many immigration and unemployment problems.

Since we are a vocational college, it would be nice to say that because of having the opportunity to work with their hands, students do not cause any problems. Unfortunately, this is not so. In Finland trainees do a lot of real work, they build real houses, for example, and in the college we have a bakery, two shops, and a restaurant where the students can gain practice. Moreover, the in-company work periods are increasing. But the most important problems in the college are related to learning difficulties, general restlessness and non-attendance.

For this reason, the need today in the college is to realise that the students have different ways of learning and individual needs within the learning process. One of our main goals is to develop more flexible and individual teaching methods to be able to help the students to get a diploma and a job.

To cater for these special needs, a whole new way of thinking is necessary by the teachers and other educational staff. It takes time. And it is not possible to attain it without a full understanding and commitment from the management.

The prevention of social exclusion is the aim of the whole college. To achieve this we have a student welfare group which meets regularly. It is a multi-professional group consisting of principal, deputy, school nurse, social counsellors and advisors. Furthermore, for preventing exclusion, various kinds of measures and projects are necessary. The most important ones are the Instruction for Life project, the Learning Centre, the Topspin project and Further Education for Teachers.

The Instruction for Life project is carried out through courses in pilot colleges. The approach to study and life is cognitive and problem-solving. The guidance given in these courses aims at supporting the formation of a positive self-image and motivating adolescents to examine their own behaviour and change it if they are not satisfied with it. The ideas produced by the students themselves are essential.

In vocational colleges over 20 % of students are dyslexic.

The Learning Centre is intended for students with learning difficulties, mostly difficulties in reading and writing which clash with their other talents and learning skills.

The dyslexia can be non-verbal, so it may affect tasks other than reading and writing. It may affect observation and memory functions. It may result in clumsiness and difficulty in thinking, in maths, mastering terms or foreign languages. Such difficulties may exist in varying combinations and dyslexics often have emotional and social difficulties.

The Learning Centre is a peaceful comfortable place with drapes, flowers and comfortable armchairs. There are a few computers with suitable programs, easy books, other materials and an able instructor. The aim is to strengthen self-esteem, to find one's own way of learning through self expression, discussion, interviews and tests.

To facilitate the learning process various equipment is used: computer programs for dyslexia, word-processing, networking, sound equipment, headsets, microphones, and video editing facilities. The Learning Centre is based on the Feuerstein method. The basis is that the experience of success is gradually transferred to more difficult tasks.

To sum up, the use of different learning styles is applied at two levels: the premises, equipment and personal guidance. And secondly the support of the whole college community.

A third important project is Topspin. This is a three-year Leonardo da Vinci pilot project aiming at developing an assessment procedure with matching support strategies for students with moderate learning difficulties.

Firstly, it concerns integrating students with special needs into the mainstream courses. Secondly it is about creating patterns to detect the students' problems during mainstream courses and to prevent their exclusion.

The Topspin project is divided into four parts. The first is the Minimum Needs Identification. It's aim is to define the students' special needs and difficulties as soon as possible in order to find out if the student can be transferred from a special group into the main group. Once in the mainstream group the aim is to find out who needs special support and in which subjects.

The Minimum Needs Identification is carried out by several teachers at the same time: the student has vocational tests given by vocational teachers, with literacy, numeracy and reading tests being given by the Finnish language teacher and by the maths teacher. If any problems arise after these tests, the student will be interviewed by the social counsellor and social advisor and the school nurse may be consulted.

The second step is creating suitable support strategies for the student. The third step is following the learning process and monitoring how the support strategies work. This is called the Monitoring System. The last step is providing further education for the teachers and other school staff.

The Topspin project is based on the idea that the integration of those with special education needs into to the mainstream, reduces exclusion and the feeling of inequality experienced by students with special needs, and furthermore supports the transfer to working life.

When different kinds of individuals study and work together it increases tolerance and understanding between both them and the educational staff. It is also important to improve the level of special needs pedagogy among teachers as the number of students with all types of problems increases all the time.

International cooperation in this project has broadened our idea of special needs pedagogy but also of pedagogy in general. It has been encouraging to realise that we are doing all right. It has given the college a new kind of know-how, reporting to Brussels, managing finances, etc.

We believe that a systematic identification of problems and strengths as well as planning support strategies in advance and a systematic assessment of the effects of such strategies can really improve everyday life in the college. Therefore the system created by this project will now be extended to every class in the college. In this way we shall be able to respond to the needs of not only special students but to the needs of every student in a more individual and flexible manner.

Finally, I have placed the further education for teachers last here. However, it could equally come first, since it is the key to all developmental actions in the college.

It is not always easy to make teachers, just like students, understand that training is for their own good and that it is necessary for every one of them. Sometimes it is just too easy to hide in the classroom and refuse to see that the education is more than just teaching the subject, the way it has always been done, regardless of the students.

However, a commitment to further development from the teachers is essential for the progress of the college. Through having different kinds of projects going on, little by little there is progress.

In fact, when a study of developmental needs of the educational staff was carried out in the college in 1995, the main result was that the teachers felt they needed further education. They preferred it to be arranged in several different ways. They wanted it as a whole unit, together with other colleges, in teams, as well as individually in the evenings and week-ends. The main condition for further education was for it to be arranged methodically and systematically. The teachers have now received special needs training, Feuerstein training and multi-cultural pedagogy.

The staff has now understood that developmental work, like development of the curricula, as well as the rotation of tasks and a division of labour and organisation are at the same time a maturation process for the staff themselves.

As the students change, the teacher's role changes too. We have more and more students whose Finnish is poor, more and more optional courses, an expanding learning environment. The teacher's role is changing to being more instructive and consultative, more of a coach. Therefore teachers need a real contact with working life and a real knowledge of teenage culture and way of life.

In vocational colleges we can see that student development is going in two opposite directions. If nothing is done, it will become more and more divided into two categories. In the first group are those who are doing well and in the second are those who are not.

From Agenda 2000 we grasp that we need flexible, creative people, who are able to learn and change occupations. But where do such people come from?

In the Helsinki Roihuvuori Vocational College we try to get adolescents to understand that without a diploma they cannot find a job. They have to realise that even though it is not always fun to wake up in the morning and go to school, and that although hanging out with friends or playing video games is much more fun, education is indispensable for their future. Giving up school for any reason is often the first step to exclusion. Problems at home, or learning difficulties do not, of course, motivate a student. However, some of these problems can be solved, if action is taken soon enough the student can get a diploma and has a chance of getting a job or further education. For this reason, measures for preventing exclusion at college level are needed.

Although now there are tools for preventing exclusion at college level, the problem of exclusion is not solved. We cannot prevent problems from arising. All we can is to make their consequences as small as possible.

Workshop 1

What teaching methods for the integration of young people in difficulty?

Summary of the two sessions on this topic on 7 and 8 May

Christine Faucqueur — Ministry of Education (F)
Eeva-Kaisa Linna — AIKE International,
network of Finnish Vocational Adult Education Centres (FIN)

The vast subject of teaching methods is a key aspect of the integration of disadvantaged young people. There was considerable interest in the workshop which was attended by a large number of people. This made it difficult, even impossible, to establish any real dialogue, but the diversity of the group made it possible, however, to look at many aspects of the topic and in particular to touch on the issues that it raises.

Experiences: three examples

The discussion was opened by three reports.

Eva Sondergaard (Denmark) described a project including a number of experiments all intended to help disadvantaged young people. Among these, a three-year training scheme for young foreigners had three objectives:

- to enable entry into the labour market,
- to provide supplementary training,
- to promote social integration.

David Horsburg (United Kingdom) presented a project supported by Socrates on the use of multimedia to help young 16 to 19-year-olds to acquire basic skills. Multimedia was chosen because of its ability to provide answers that are tailored to everyone's specific learning needs.

Lastly, Eeva Laurila (Finland), described the experiments conducted by a vocational training college. Their main feature was the preliminary analysis of each student's method of learning and as a corollary their specific needs in order to pinpoint tailored teaching solutions.

Teaching methods

While they may appear different, these experiments share certain teaching strategies:

- building up young people's confidence and self-esteem so that young people can rebuild their self-image which may have been tarnished by what has happened in the past;
- motivating them by choosing activities, projects or resources (multimedia, for instance) that young people enjoy and involving them in this choice;
- personalising training in order to meet each young person's specific needs;
- adapting the pace of learning to each learner;
- remediation;
- listening, counselling and guidance;
- mediation.

Other dimensions appeared in specific ways in one or other of the presentations:

- working with families whose mobilisation is an important aspect of the Danish project;
- detailed evaluation of every young person's learning profiles and needs and ways of making young people themselves aware of these profiles and needs;
- the creation of evaluation and even self-evaluation tools.

Some key questions

The workshop discussions during the sessions of 7 and 8 May took place at various times. The discussion focused firstly on a number of basic questions and highlighted a number of problematic areas:

- the problem of reconciling personally tailored learning with group work;
- ways of structuring knowledge and learning in very free learning contexts;
- evaluation of the methods used and resources chosen;
- the problems that teachers face in meeting the twofold — educational and technological — challenge posed by multimedia;
- the need to construct partnerships with parents, associations, etc., to take account of the major influence that experience and learning outside school has on young people;
- the need to develop tutoring, counselling, listening and guidance on practices and to improve teachers' abilities in these areas.

Routes towards networking

The workshop also identified areas for common work and 10 or so project leaders said that they were willing to cooperate: personal pathways, analysis of the causes of marginalisation and exclusion, the values linked to work, adapting training methods to these values and young people's culture, partnerships and the integration of schools into their environment.

Personal pathways

There are major constraints on the personalisation of training pathways, even though individual routes for young people are now common practice. Validating very complex experience is problematic and requires a great deal of management; nor should the cost of this be forgotten. Personalisation therefore needs to be examined in greater depth, especially as young people are often more interested in learning in a group, highlighting the fact that the learning of knowledge has a social side.

The causes of marginalisation and exclusion

Young people are too often subject to opprobrium when they encounter problems: we tend to forget that society's problems and the constraints that it imposes on these young people, for instance the fact that there are too few job vacancies or that the educational system is not flexible enough, may be at the root of these problems.

The values attached to work

These values are changing. Nowadays, the growth of the 'third sector', part-time work and temporary jobs has meant that finding a 'normal' job is no longer the only option. This may have major consequences when defining training pathways and developing teaching methods.

Taking account of young people's values and culture

Young people often build their own society around their own values and even their own language with language codes that trainers must understand. Account needs to be taken of this when formulating pathways and choosing which methods to use: training has to reflect young people's experiences and interests and convert these into projects through which they can realise themselves.

Partnerships and the integration of schools into their environments

Integrating young people into society was one of the key issues highlighted by the experiments presented at the workshop. In some cases local authorities and local agencies have set up projects or groups specifically designed to support the employment of disadvantaged young people by small and medium-sized enterprises. Financial incentives are offered in some cases. The aim is to work with young people towards their acceptance by society: young people could themselves, for instance, carry out research into enterprise outlets for their own target group.

It was not possible, however, to explore two pertinent directions in any depth. These could be the subject of subsequent exchanges:

- penetrating further into the 'black box' of teaching methods; analysing and comparing, for instance, actual personalisation methods, types of guidance and the role that listening plays in these various schemes. Understanding what these terms actually represent — as one participant very pertinently pointed out — is more important than constructing teaching methods; these young people do not think in ways that differ from other young people;
- organising concrete cooperation on the topics tackled, between the various projects concerned and at European level. This could lead to exchanges between partners having common interests on the website that is soon to be opened.

Workshop 2

What role should the new technologies play?

Vocational information and guidance
New technologies

Christian Boeldieu
Association nationale pour la Formation des Adultes (AFPA) (F)

Vocational guidance does not try to 'impose guidance' on young people, but to help them to find the resources that they need to 'guide' themselves.

The development of multimedia and the emergence of new computer supports: CD-ROM, Minitel, the Internet, etc., mean that everyone now has direct access to a whole range of information; this is tending to generate new problems of comprehension since an excess of information often leads to confusion because of its saturation effects on a relatively inexperienced public.

Computer users normally work in an intuitive way and try to locate specific information rather than exploring information methodically. When searching a database, for instance, they try first to satisfy a need by attempting to locate 'what they need' rather than exhaustively consulting 'what there is'.

In order to help searchers to carry out documentary searches about jobs and training, their needs and concerns need to be directly targeted and they need to be helped to formalise their tastes and centres of interest and to discover, over and above their abilities or knowledge, what personal interests they can take into account when making their choice of career.

It quickly became evident that personal interest questionnaires, intended to simplify information searches, seemed to be resources particularly in keeping with computer supports.

Young people also seem to find computers more 'credible' than other traditional supports, unfortunately sometimes excessively so.

In the relationships that guidance counsellors forge with young people, the starting point has to be their ideas or dreams (however Utopian they may be) and not their frustrations. They need to say 'I would like' rather than 'I must!'

Using tests as a support for their thinking helps young people to formalise their thoughts and then to develop them with the help of the guidance counsellor and thus to take an active part in formulating their own career plans. The answers that they give are in no way final. They are no more than pointers that young people can explore with their interlocutors in order to help them to discover whether they actually possess the qualities and resources provided by certain centres of interest that can be put to use in a job.

The way in which answers are formulated should also try to take away any fear of punishment, make the most of people and give them back their dynamism using language with which they are familiar. Young people who are insecure or who have failed at school need to be encouraged to take a positive view since this is the first step towards helping them to construct their future.

It was on the basis of these considerations that the *'Métier qui me plaît'* (My kind of job) vocational guidance test program was designed in cooperation with AFPA.

The *'Métier qui me plaît'*
Vocational guidance test program

The *Métier qui me plaît* program enables young people to prepare for job interviews by helping them to express their centres of interest and to illustrate them using examples drawn from their daily lives.

It starts from a basic test which leads on to various specialist sub-tests.

The basic test

The basic test takes the form of a questionnaire with 30 items each of which has six options.

Each option is associated with one of the following six profiles:

- **A. Sports and nature**
- **B. Arts and literature**
- **C. Communications and social services**
- **D. Science and technology**
- **E. Administration and management**
- **F. Enterprise and business**

A comparison of these profiles with other vocational guidance test typologies and in particular with the theory of J. Holland, an American psychologist at the Johns Hopkins University in Baltimore, who proposes a classification of occupations deduced from a set of considerations on occupational choice, makes it possible to draw up the following table of correspondence.

The subtests

In a traditional 'paper-based' test, where a question paper and an answer sheet are needed, a large number of questions (items) have to be asked in order to be able to explore all centres of interest.

Correspondence of the 'Metier qui me plaît' profiles with other interest questionnaires

Kuder scale	Strong scale	Guilford factor	Holland typology	C.r.a.s.e.o. de Benedetto	Metier qui me plaît
Open air mechanical	Aviator	Mechanical	Realistic	Concrete	Sport and nature
Scientific	Physicist	Scientific	Investigative	Research	Science and technology
Artistic, musical, literary	Musician	Aesthetic	Artistic	Artistic	Arts and literature
Social service	Teachers of musical sciences	Social service	Social	Social	Social service and com- munication
Persuasive	Head of sales	Enterprise	Entrepreneurial	Enterprise	Enterprise and business
Calculation, office work	Accountant	Office	Conventional	Organisation	Administration and management

Computer processing now makes it possible to work in stages; the '*Métier qui me plaît*' sub-tests take the form of a range of interdependent branches exploring personal interests not just from the point of view of initial guidance but also from the point of view of further guidance in a particular sector (bearing in mind the person's knowledge and experience).

Each of the subtests always suggests bridges with the other subtests. This interactive configuration makes it possible to pinpoint centres of interest so that they can then be expressed in all the occupational sectors.

The '*Métier qui me plaît*' includes seven subtests corresponding to the various profiles of the basic test.

General organisation of the program

The '*Métier qui me plaît*' offers:

- 140 items (multiple-choice questions)
  575 proposals
  70 different profiles/subprofiles
  400 job sheets indexed by interest keys.
- A graphical representation of the results that breaks down the answers given so that they can be more readily interpreted by a specialist.
- Links to all other documentary resources (ANPE, ONISEP, AFPA and CIDJ).

The questionnaire

The items are divided into four standard questionnaire categories relating to:

- **Emotional and social identification**
- **Occupational perceptions**
- **Social perceptions**
- **Centres of interest.**

Emotional and social identification

The initial questions invite the respondent to imagine 'if you were?'

They are presented in the form of a game with which the child is already likely to be familiar. This approach often makes it possible to remove any fears that teenagers may have about a questionnaire whose purpose is not entirely clear to them. They are shown from the outset that the questionnaire is about them and what they think and not what people think of them. The game approach also helps diffident or anxious respondents gradually to enter into the spirit of the test and gradually to express more personal feelings.

From the point of view of their content, some questions use icons which may in some cases be the only way in which respondents can express particularly complex emotional situations.

Occupational perceptions

There is nothing empirical about the way in which teenagers perceive a job. Their image of a job is based on what they have heard which they will interpret as good or bad depending on the satisfaction or frustration that adults have expressed about their jobs.

These questions initially create an awareness of their environment with the result that young people will then try to find out, for instance, whether a job is carried out alone or as a team, outside or in an office, whether it is active or sedentary, etc. They will look for similarities with those jobs of which they have had personal experience or of which their friends have had experience in work placements or seasonal work.

Social perceptions

Social perceptions do not obey any tangible rule. They are shaped by each individual's family, cultural, social and political history. They change constantly as time passes and differ from one country to another. The test items dealing with social perceptions are therefore based on subjective perceptions of job success and the place that young people imagine that they can occupy in society.

Centres of interest

The key importance that centres of interest play in occupational choices and the fact that they are often neglected in favour of performance, abilities and knowledge provides the justification for this test. The questionnaire therefore explores respondents' personal experiences of daily life looking at leisure, entertainment and memories of school.

Presentation of answers

'What would you like to be when you grow up?'

While the process of vocational guidance starts in infancy by asking children to imagine 'What would you like to be?', as they grow older there is a shift towards the negative: 'You can't do that job!'

A whole range of reasons is advanced: not good enough at maths, bad sight, too many people taking those options, sector at risk, too old, etc. This leads children, who started with a number of ideas in mind, to say, when the time comes to choose what they want to do, 'I don't know' or rather 'I don't know any more', since any job plans, like their illusions, have gone by the board with the result that they have gradually started to fail at school.

Using information to 're-open' the door of what is possible is the first step that needs to be taken.

Guidance counsellors are well aware of this problem. While there are hundreds of trades, young people become unable to quote more than one or two. How can they be encouraged to take a new interest in their future and how can dialogue be promoted between young people and counsellors so that they can work together to resolve the problems that guidance raises?

It is by starting from what they would like to, and what they envisage they can, put into a job that they will find an answer. Being able to talk about oneself makes it possible to pinpoint one 'is' and then to find out what one can 'do'.

New technologies in training programmes for disadvantaged young people in the city of Cologne (Volkshochschule)

Diethelm Jeske
AMT für Weiterbildung
Volkshochschule, Köln (D)

Ladies and gentlemen,

I wish to talk about the use of new technology in a field that is becoming ever more important as the unemployment of young people increases, posing a serious threat to the cohesion of European society. I wish to talk about vocational guidance, on-the-job and bringing-up-to-level training aimed at young people who wish to gain access to the world of work. Therefore I shall cover the practical use of microcomputers as a teaching tool, the use of PCs in counselling and vocational guidance and lastly I shall describe school exemplariness in terms of its equipment.

Information technology (IT) skills are key qualifications and need to be looked at from four points of view: first the content of the subject, i.e., information technology itself. Second, IT cannot be an isolated entity, rather IT skills should be taught by combining it with other subjects. Third, the integrating aspect of IT for those involved in vocational training. And fourth, IT should be taught using activity based approaches.

The IT competence I wish to talk about goes far beyond the acquisition of purely technical skills. What I understand by IT skills is providing young people with the chance, the ability and the qualifications to use this new media as a springboard to emancipate themselves and to find a place in society through their own innovative and creative potential. Part of such qualifications are strategic and cultural skills, as well as the ability to reflect and make rational choices.

What we need to reach these aims is openness, a willingness to make use of new ways of learning and new ways of working in schools and other areas of education, particularly vocational guidance and counselling, yet without discarding the traditional concepts. The old and the new ways of learning and teaching will interact: new methods will put traditional ones to the test and assist them in renewing and reforming themselves. The course will become more of a learning workshop in which participants independently discover the content of the particular field which interests them. Thus, perhaps, a long standing pedagogical requirement can at last be fulfilled: a learning style that combines independence with discovery. The new way of learning will become more important than methods directed by a teacher using school books and a curriculum. Many things can be learned more easily with the help of the Internet and multimedia. Let me give you some examples:

- Multimedia fosters a systematic access to all types of knowledge (because it increases curiosity, it motivates, it provides new ways of accessing important information, it provides new ways of solving problems, it helps in learning how to learn).
- Multimedia fosters independent learning (because training methods and learning speeds are individual, via the Internet, trainees can work on shared tasks without any regard for the physical distance separating them).
- Multimedia promotes interdisciplinary learning (because information from various subjects can be readily combined).
- Multimedia fosters greater global and intercultural understanding (because e-mail provides direct communication in an authentic linguistic and cultural context).
- Multimedia fosters a dynamic knowledge.
- Multimedia promotes social skills (since tasks have to be solved through communication skills and teamwork).

- Multimedia promotes a widening of perspectives and tolerance (because beneficiaries can access the entire world via the Internet).

By using such postulates, we in Cologne involved in vocational training, guidance and counselling, are deploying this new medium. There are four basic functions:

1. as a production tool, for word processing, etc.;
2. as a teaching and learning tool supporting the learning process;
3. as a means of communication;
4. as a means of acquiring information.

The PC is a highly flexible medium that broadens teaching methods and motivates participants. Due to this, we use the microcomputers not only in the computer sciences themselves but in all other subjects too.

1. The PC as a teaching tool

A few words on how PCs may be used as a teaching medium in vocational training and general education.

Beneficiary oriented training provides a good framework for the use of a microcomputers. Experience shows that participants enjoy working with PCs. Learners who have difficulty acquiring new knowledge obtain better results due to the motivational aspects provided by the PC. Most beneficiaries feel a personal enhancement due to modern image of the computer and because the majority of them do not have a PC at home. Another positive aspect is that young people are not afraid of this tool, they already have positive experience with new technology through video games played in their leisure time. From a psychological point of view, the learner does not feel compromised when he makes a mistake, a computer is infinitely more patient than classmates or an instructor and this new learning atmosphere increases the learner's readiness to try out new ways of solving problems, by making mistakes and then learning through correcting them.

One of the major problems with young people is their lack of concentration. Here again, by its very presence, the computer requires the pupil to concentrate consistently.

Individual learning thus becomes possible. If we use well-structured learning applications, each learner can seek and find the tasks that are suited to his particular level of skills. Tests carried out in recent years clearly show that young people are reassured when finding tasks that they can accomplish. The degree of difficulty is adapted to a learning curve without requiring a teacher in the background to determine the speed of learning. The teacher becomes more of a course moderator.

Good teaching programs provide a sense of accomplishment and stimulus through the successful completion of a series of progressive steps. This enables longer and more concentrated periods of work. The programs must, of course, be both interesting and varied and provide different levels of difficulty. A good example of usable training software is NIPPES.

In school subjects, we only make use of computers when good software is available; in this way we avoid over-stressing those with learning difficulties.

For practice and knowledge consolidation, the computer is unbeatable. Teachers can concentrate on the slowest learners and problems can be approached more directly. The faster learners work individually using the in-built help function provided by the program.

This raises a question: where exactly should we make use of computers? I believe, first in subjects requiring many different exercise levels. Maths, languages and bringing-up-to-level in writing skills are all areas in which beneficiaries can benefit through the use of PCs. This is also the case with school leavers preparing for the world of work. Here, a lot has to be absorbed in a short time and the computer is an ideal tool for such an intensive learning process.

Equally, school subjects such as biology, sociology and applied science can be illustrated and presented. In applied sciences, pupils can work with simple programs that simulate the control of equipment, in biology the functions of the body or evolutionary processes can be displayed or simulated, in sociology, learners can make use of the German Parliament web site to access sources of pertinent information.

To summarise, one can say that the computer can be used in every field of knowledge and learning when good and suitable teaching software is either available or can be produced by the trainer. Fears that participants will not the learn basic skills of writing, reading and communication are misplaced. Though teaching may be done with the help of a computer, there will always be other fields in which the traditional basic skills are needed and practised. The successes made possible for the student by the computer create a willingness to deal with other new and more difficult content.

With the aid of multimedia programs specialised computer knowledge is not required.

2. The potential of the computer in vocational guidance and counselling

How can we best make use of this new medium in vocational guidance and counselling?

To discover what young people undergoing vocational guidance and training are interested in and for which profession they are best suited, the vocational counselling staff in our institution construct vocational training paths. They obtain data by observing learners during courses and store their findings in databases providing a detailed view of the whole vocational guidance process. All counselling and pedagogical staff are equipped with computers allowing them to construct training paths, update information and integrate additional information from external sources on the Internet and from other organisations web sites.

Another tool in discovering learners' interests and abilities are the CD–ROM provided by other organisations, such as the Cologne Labour Office. These help complete our view of what is possible for the particular individual.

Information technology is employed by major institutions like the German Labour Office. It is something that people seeking access to work need to know about and be able to use. We want them to be able to use such offers posted on the Internet or various Intranets. The completeness and relevance of such employment information has a remarkable advantage when compared to traditional print media. It offers two kinds of information: general information on occupations, and concrete job offers. Furthermore, e-mail then makes it easier to contact enterprises or schools.

Let us not forget, too, that this medium equally helps produce professional-looking job applications which can be later perfected and updated without frustration by pupils with learning difficulties.

Our hardware

Lastly, I would like to describe how our school in Cologne is equipped.

We want our learners to make use of our equipment in several ways.

There are two classrooms entirely reserved for teaching information technology. In these classrooms, all PCs are networked and have access to the Internet. There are three other classrooms equipped with three PCs each. These PCs are equally networked and have access to the Internet.

There is a room in which nine computers can be used as work stations for either individual or group work. This room will be used for internal and external videoconferencing. Lastly, there are four computers that learners can use in order to do homework or prepare texts.

And what of the teacher in all of this?

The basis for all these activities is the teachers knowledge of the subject and his or her willingness to work with new media. Traditional ideas of teaching and conveying knowledge are changing. This means coping with the individual's personal fears about computers, and entails learning how to teach using PCs. Consequently a new understanding of the teacher's role, how to approach the computer and use it in vocational guidance and training is necessary if we want to use this new medium successfully. Producing an overall concept should identify problems on the one hand, and advantages and necessary changes on the other.

New technologies: putting the learner in control

Bronwen Robinson
Lifeskills International Ltd (UK)

We know that exclusion, creating a deeply divided society, is impossible to sustain without huge human and economic cost. Exclusion creates a society that is not only expensive, but highly volatile. If exclusion is expensive economically, looked at from a human perspective, one of individual right, fulfilment and contribution to society, it is untenable. Individuals faced with exclusion cannot and will not fulfil their potential. This is the challenge governments are facing — how to move individuals from the excluded state into one of inclusion.

Many research projects and experiences have highlighted that the golden key to achieve inclusion is education. Yet, whilst education may be the golden key, at the same time much of the process of developing feelings of exclusion can be related to the classroom experience. This is particularly exacerbated where the experience of school has been unsuccessful, if not a disaster in terms of experience and qualification attainment. This experience coupled with, and often fuelled by, a poverty of aspiration means they become a 'lost generation' — a generation excluded from active citizenship, economic well-being and a generation of passive recipients of benefits with the dependency that results. For many individuals throughout the UK and in other countries the poverty that entraps them means that there seems no prospect of change or escape. They see excitement in things and ways of life that do not meet society's norms. Without socially acceptable ways to progress they may be pushed into anti-social patterns where education and training is seen as irrelevant. Education and training has failed not so much because of the quality of the delivery, but more as a result of the curricular design and the mode of delivery being geared towards the norm of participation. For individuals where that norm is beyond comprehension, the curriculum is irrelevant and the experience of learning, first time, is disastrous. To offer these individuals yet more of the same, more classroom delivered learning, is not the solution. It has failed once, the prognosis is that unless relevance is addressed, unless the experience feels and is perceived to be significantly different for the learner, it will fail again. This relevance and new way of delivery is the opportunity that new technologies can offer.

Used most effectively the key aspects relating to the use of technology in learning are:

- The learner is in control as opposed to the teacher being the disciplinarian classroom manager.
- Getting the mind to work as opposed to the computer giving the answer — avoiding the magic-box syndrome.
- Develop learning and thinking exercises based on self-discovery rather than the more traditional listening, watching and copying.
- Freedom for the individual to construct their learning in the personal learning domain.
- The use of learning stations that provide feedback but do not make judgment.

It is this dynamic, learner-centred approach which is at the heart of Citizen Connect. Harnessing the power of the Internet, Citizen Connect is an integrated development tool providing individuals with an on-line resource providing information, guidance and support in their quest to find work, careers and become a life-long learner. In short, Citizen Connect is using knowledge and technology for social inclusion by targeting on employment and employability.

Citizen Connect is a joint venture between Lifeskills International (UK) and Axia Multi Media Corporation (Canada). The key focus of our approach is:

- Helping unemployed persons to enter or even return to the world of work through systematic understanding of their needs, interests, values and available opportunities.
- Helping individuals to discover the relevance of learning for employment and be able to plan and access educational and learning opportunities.

Our strategy is to integrate information technology with existing mentoring and coaching systems to provide faster, more individualised and custom responses to individual needs.

It is important to recognise the opportunities technology brings, but also the limits. We recognise that collective learning and human intervention are important resources for the learner. Within the design it is not intended to replace the role of the career advisor or counsellor, but complement and add to the options open to people who need help to shape their future. It is designed to empower the users to take personal responsibility for the development of their skills, their job progression and their future. It is a 'help' system designed to be used regularly, routinely, at points of crisis and unexpected change through the changing patterns of employment.

To date, we are in active discussions within the UK, in Canada and within Europe. Citizen Connect will be piloted in five key regions in the UK as part of the Welfare to Work programme for young people called the New Deal. It will also be piloted within the Second Chance School in Leeds. Leeds, in common with the UK Government, believe that fundamental to the successful inclusion of young people is employment. Their vision, in line with the Government's, is to create an inclusive society, characterised by full employment, a flexible labour market, a dynamic and creative economy which embraces technology and creates a culture of lifelong learning for all. Citizen Connect is positioned to help achieve that vision.

Workshop 2

What role should the new technologies play?

Summary of the two sessions on this topic on 7 and 8 May

Eddy Adams
Institute for Social and Economic Research (INSER) (UK)
Jacques Jansen
Centrum voor Europese Studies en Opleidingen
(CESO Consultants) (NL)

This workshop looked at the role that the new technologies can play in the re-integration of disadvantaged young people and highlighted five main issues:

1. Helping young people to learn to learn.
2. Transforming the ways in which education is organised.
3. Forging new relationships between trainers and young trainees.
4. Easing access to the working world.
5. Introducing efficient solutions into education systems without diminishing the quality of the education supply.

A number of pertinent questions arose out of these issues: Why use multimedia technologies for this target group? Are they not being used simply because everyone else is using them? Because they are fashionable?

The workshop looked at three examples to find answers to these questions.

'Lifeskills International' provided the first example with its presentation of the 'Citizen project' for multimedia guidance on future career choices. The project has been designed to help young people to take control of their lives and to make their own decisions with the help of a set of support services including the acquisition of key qualifications, job-finding skills and an understanding of the nature of current job vacancies in the labour market.

The second example was provided by ABM's *'Arbeit und Lernen'* project which places the stress on the identified functions of the new technologies in education and training, especially knowledge learning and communication tools — as well as the technological tools that provide access to this actual communication. The use of computers seems to help young people to take an interactive approach for which they have to take responsibility themselves and that cannot simply be taught; using computers helps them to find new answers to problems and the trainer becomes more a mediator or facilitator; an integrated approach needs to be taken to what is taught and the use of the resource.

The third example was the software package called *'Le métier qui me plaît'* created by AFPA. After finding out about young people's profiles and centres of interest, potential career profiles are drawn up. This strategy takes a global approach to young people, their perception of their role in society, their abilities and their interests. In this case the new technologies are used to refine the approach and to eliminate unnecessary questions.

By way of conclusion, it would seem that the new technologies are resources of considerable potential for the education and training of our target groups, but that some risks may be involved: some young people may, for instance, become increasingly isolated and idiosyncratic, unless this is offset by providing them with social and collective skills. It should be borne in mind that technology is no more than a tool serving the fight against social exclusion.

The workshop finally put forward five recommendations:

1. The Commission needs to establish an effective Intranet and Internet network for the first and second strands; it should ensure, however, that the network is properly managed and that service is continuous, as otherwise chaos will reign. The network must be genuinely accessible and we must learn to use it efficiently.
2. There is a major need for technologies tailored specifically to disadvantaged young people who are excluded. There has been a great deal of criticism of existing software. The Commission should support the development and production of new tailored 'packages' and the adaptation of existing packages.
3. We should think about new forms of cooperation between the public and private sectors. Public or semi-public sector costs are high. Once again, it is up to the Commission to take action to clarify the conditions under which these software packages are marketed (contractual conditions, copyright, distribution methods, wages and royalties, profit-sharing).
4. There is major problem with the training of trainers and tutors, the costs of which may in some cases account for as much as 90 % of investment costs.
5. The Commission could also support further research and in particular active research into the new technologies. Better use could, for instance, be made of commercially available computer games and other packages (such as encyclopaedias) as teaching aids. There is not enough funding to develop new products and prior research and testing is needed.

Once these recommendations had been formulated, the workshop participants expressed a great deal of satisfaction with the opportunity that they had had for discussion which had been of great interest, in terms of ideas, experiences and products, for those working on concrete schemes. They thanked the European Commission for organising this conference and hoped that this kind of exchange could continue in the future.

Workshop 3

Objectives and methods of validation and certification of skills

Objectives and methods for validation and certification of skills
UK case study: Rewarding and widening achievement: the ASDAN initiative

David Brockington
ASDAN (UK)

The case study will identify the basic social and pedagogic functions of assessment. These will be analysed in comparison with the ASDAN case study initiative. There are currently 120 000 learners registered annually on ASDAN programmes from over 2 000 centres. The majority of these are from UK secondary schools (11-18 age range) and UK colleges of further education (16+ age range).

ASDAN programmes make a unique contribution in the area of personal, social, health and moral education (PSHME) in offering individual and group challenges to students, together with certificated rewards for their successful completion. This process of learning based upon formative assessment, action planning and review of progress, is found to be highly motivating, relevant to students' perceived needs and instrumental in delivering the UK deficit of the key skills within defined curriculum contexts. The recent research findings on assessment approaches from Paul Black and Dylan Williams at Kings College, London, on assessment regimes will be considered in the case study.

ASDAN is approved by DFEE (the UK Ministry of Education) as one of the nationally permitted routes for the teaching and accreditation of key skills to the pre-16 age group.

For the post-16 age group the Awards as they embody key skills are also approved by the DFEE. The case study will identify the current UK definition of key skills.

The case study will identify that the ASDAN Award Scheme is genuinely comprehensive in its coverage from those with special learning needs to those learners seeking university entrance. The case study will consider the features of assessment built into the design of the ASDAN programmes and how they assist learners.

The ASDAN scheme has the UK Confederation of British Industry (CBI) endorsement.

Over 130 institutions of higher education in the UK now formally endorse the higher level of the ASDAN Awards known as the (Universities Award). Mention is made by the UK Universities and Colleges Admissions Service (UCAS) in its guidance to candidates for entry to higher education.

An independent evaluation by the London University Institute of Education has concluded that ASDAN has a significant role to play in the delivery of the broad range of key skills within the emerging national framework of UK qualifications pre- and post-16.

This independent evaluation summary from the London University Institute of Education is also attached.

Key skills and the ASDAN Award Schemes

Introduction

In 1997, at the invitation of the ASDAN management team, the Post-16 Education Centre at the Institute of Education, University of London conducted an evaluation of the ASDAN Award Schemes. We examined the context in which key skills have come to play a prominent, though problematic, role in the post-compulsory phase of education and training in this country. Drawing attention both to the strengths of the Award Schemes and ways in which the scheme could benefit from further development, we concluded that the schemes provide flexible and versatile vehicles for teaching and learning key skills, and for their assessment and accreditation.

1. Views from the schools and colleges

We gathered data from our evaluation, in particular, from a series of interviews that we conducted with teachers and managers in a sample of schools and colleges in the London area.

Teachers and managers see the flexibility of the ASDAN Award Schemes as a major advantage. They use the award schemes in a number of ways. Frequently they provide the teaching and accreditation framework for a range of curriculum activities that are not covered in formally examined courses. In many schools this is the personal and social education (PSE or PSHE) programme or the tutorial programme of European work experience. In other centres the ASDAN scheme provides accreditation for courses designed to meet the needs of particular groups of students, such as those with learning difficulties or for students with English as a second language.

Teachers value the way that the design of the scheme allows the student's key skills learning to take place in a realistic context, one which is defined and developed jointly by teacher and student. This is important while the division between academic and vocational qualifications remains. Practitioners consider that, unlike other key skills schemes, ASDAN schemes are explicitly designed to overcome this divide, and thus support teachers dealing with the day-to-day problems arising from it.

The accreditation and certification that are part of the scheme and, therefore, recognition for progression are seen as an advantage of the scheme. There are several reasons for this. For A-level students and others seeking higher education entrance, an ASDAN Award is regarded as a way of demonstrating the student's breadth of experience to HE providers. The Award Scheme is given recognition in the UCAS application process. In this respect, accreditation itself becomes a motivating factor. Both students and staff are quite instrumental, and an ASDAN award is seen as giving added value to a higher education application form. Finally, funding is important in the FE sector, since colleges can receive funding for providing the ASDAN award.

Our limited survey proved to be a rich source of data, reflecting many of the main issues in the national debate on key skills, and it afforded the additional insights of teachers attempting to deliver them. What emerges is a series of tensions which teachers — and students — have to live with, and which the ASDAN team will need to continue to consider carefully. These are the tensions between:

- The desire for flexibility in curriculum design, and the need for guidance on content.
- The need for learning expectations to be clearly defined, and the need for learning activities to take place in a context which has some intrinsic value.
- The external pressures for rigorous accreditation and the need for local interpretation and individual initiative.
- The need for flexible ways of demonstrating achievement and the increased workload and resulting paperwork and paper chase.
- The requirement for more staff development and the pressure on staff time.

2. A summary of the Institute of Education's evaluation

Curriculum

The ASDAN key skills curriculum is based on a set of distinct principles, which value the professionalism of the teacher and encourage the active participation of the student.

ASDAN's curriculum principles can be described as follows:

- Education, and therefore the curriculum, should be concerned with the development of the whole person.

- Personal, social, practical and vocational skills should be valued alongside academic achievement and should therefore be developed and accredited.
- For key skills, teachers working closely with their students are best placed to develop a curriculum that is relevant and responsive to individual and local needs.
- Students and teachers are motivated and empowered through involvement in managing the learning process.

Development of the whole person

The student population in Britain today, particularly for those staying on post-16, is very diverse and, for many young people, the traditional academic curriculum appears to have little relevance. Even those students who are, on the face of it, successfully engaging with academic study often face this problem. In this situation motivation and relevance become the main issues for teachers and of course, for students. The challenges defined in the ASDAN curriculum with their direct links to the demands of the adult world, go some way towards addressing these issues.

Valuing a wide range of achievement

The scheme places value on academic work, but also on personal, social, practical and vocational achievement. This is directly linked to issues of motivation and relevance. The ASDAN schemes cut across traditional subject boundaries and provide a curriculum framework that values skills that are not easily encompassed by other qualifications. In this way, it fosters the development of shared values and ways of relating to others both in school and in the wider community. The scheme is also flexible enough to encompass individual interests, local needs and cultural differences by encouraging activities which motivate the student, since they are chosen because they have some intrinsic value. Thus, the scheme accredits learning not recognised by more traditional qualifications.

Teacher involvement in curriculum design

The scheme is designed to be flexible and to promote teacher involvement, so as to address issues that are of interest and concern to particular individuals, schools or colleges, or in particular communities. The scope that the award provides for teachers to be involved enables them to relate the curriculum to student needs, and it both relies on and enhances their own sense of professionalism.

Active engagement of the student

The principle of active engagement of students with the planning, learning, assessment, reviewing and recording processes is important, although it seems to be more problematic in practice. The aim is to encourage the student to be involved with the learning processes in an active way that develops skills and confidence. This is an aim that most teachers seem to agree with in principle. However, the teaching and learning activities do require a clear understanding of the scheme and commitment on the part of the teacher, for example in the action planning and review phases of the students' activity. Without this preparation the scheme can get lost in paperwork and come to be regarded as something of a chore.

Most of the teachers and managers whom we interviewed share the principles outlined above. Given the onslaught on these values through the introduction of the National Curriculum and the growth of the 'competence' movement in vocational qualifications, we do not consider that principle alone can be the reason for the rapid growth of the ASDAN scheme. It is more likely that the scheme has grown in popularity because it is founded on the real needs of students (and therefore teachers) to engage in meaningful and relevant activity, and for this to be valued.

Links to other qualifications

The flexibility of the ASDAN schemes is a major advantage. The schemes can be used to articulate with other curriculum frameworks and qualifications which range from programmes of study being followed by pre-university A-level students, to programmes for students with special or language needs for whom the national curriculum is not appropriate, ASDAN has produced materials that make these links explicit for teachers.

In terms of the key skills 'Communication, Application of Number and Information Technology' recent ASDAN materials have made these more easily identifiable within the challenges and activities. This strategy appears to have been successful in that key skills are made explicit for personal review and external assessment purposes and are also developed and practised within a context.

A long-standing issue within the key skills debate is whether discrete or integrated delivery is preferable. This tension appears to reflect some confusion about what precisely 'key skills' are as the term has been used to include:

- remedying a basic skills deficit; i.e. ensuring basic competence in literacy, numeracy and IT;
- spending more curriculum time on subjects such as English and maths;
- learning a foreign language;
- 'applying' basic skills outside the classroom;
- developing the capacity to work in a team, solve problems and manage one's own learning.

Obviously these are not mutually exclusive categories but it seems clear that the final two which embody 'broader' skills require a form of curriculum delivery not encompassed by traditional qualifications.

In our view, it is in within this broad concept of key skills that ASDAN's main strength lies. Although the scheme has the capacity to accredit 'basic skills' it is unique in its approach to the delivery of broader skills.

Assessment and accreditation

In the ASDAN schemes, assessment reinforces the approach to teaching and learning, and has four main attributes. It is inclusive and flexible, it is an integral part of a formative approach to developing the students' key skills through the portfolio, and it relies on the professional judgment of the teacher.

Inclusiveness and flexibility

Assessment in the Award Scheme is inclusive in two senses. Firstly, the scheme accredits at all levels from entry level to higher education entry (at Level 3). Other schemes accredit key skills only at the basic level (pre-vocational schemes), or have proved unattractive to schools and colleges preparing students for A levels (the GNVQ key skills schemes), or are limited to mainstream A-level candidates (A/AS Level in General Studies). Secondly, the scheme accredits a wide field of the student's experience including experience gained through interests, community or voluntary activity, work experience or visits away from the neighbourhood. All such activities can count in the assessment process and be included as activities and challenges for accreditation.

A formative approach to assessment

The Award Scheme's assessment methodology comprises the successive stages of planning, activity and review in repeated cycles, and in this respect assessment is a formative part of the students' learning experience. Assessment itself forms part of the process of learning. Used effectively, the assessment process enables the student with the teacher's help to gauge his or her progress, reflect on what has been learnt, and develop and adjust subsequent steps.

Reliance on the teacher's professional judgment

Assessment, both in its formative aspect and in the decisions that are made about successful qualification for the Award at its different levels, depends strongly on the judgments made by teachers. This applies within the particular centre and at the area moderation meetings. We have no doubt that this reliance on the teachers' professionalism is one of the characteristics that accounts for the notable attractiveness of the scheme to many of the teachers and lecturers who use it and in part, for the scheme's rapid growth in recent years.

Strengthening the assessment process, through ASDAN's organisation and network

Notwithstanding its strengths, this teacher-centred approach to assessment raises difficult issues of quality control. In our full report we recommend a number of ways in which the assessment and accreditation processes can be strengthened. We do not recommend that ASDAN should move towards end of course tests, even though these can be marked objectively, nor towards a box-ticking mode of assessment; these would undermine the purposes that underpin the design of the ASDAN Award Schemes. Rather, we recommend for consideration ways that the assessment and accreditation can be strengthened through further development of the written guidelines for teachers, through developing the professional network and through further staff development and teacher induction at moderation meetings.

Teachers see the ASDN central team as responsive to their views when revising the content and format of the workbooks, and as innovative in extending the scheme to support a still wider range of learning environments. We consider that the Award Scheme could devote more attention to work experience as an area of activity and we recommend that the scheme should build on its links with the employers. In our view, the ASDAN Award Scheme could have a leading role in helping to build professional 'communities of excellence' among teachers.

We also recommend that the potential of developments in information technology — both as a means of communicating with networks of teachers and as a key skill for young people — should be exploited rapidly.

3. Conclusions

Our full report reaches a number of specific conclusions. We conclude that the particular strength of the ASDAN Award Scheme lies in its characteristic approach to the teaching and learning of key skills particularly the personal and interpersonal skills.

We recommend that the ASDAN Award Scheme achievements should be built upon through:

- Developing a module bank of assignments so that, by agreement, centres begin to use a wide range of common (or similar) for the different challenges.
- Aligning the award levels clearly with the levels in the emerging national qualifications framework.
- Improving the guidelines for moderation meetings, and encouraging all centres to work to common guidelines.
- Involving practitioners in developing exemplars of good practice linked to the guidelines.
- Extending the provision of professional development to a wider range of teachers who may be involved in delivering the Award Scheme, even if it is not a central part of their teaching.
- Extending the depth and coverage of professional development for Centre leaders, and equipping them to become Award Scheme trainers.
- Exploring the possibility of accrediting Award training within a number of masters-level programmes across the country.
- Exploring ways of using IT to develop networking between Centres using the Award, and sharing of materials between the different Centres.
- Exploring ways of increasing the involvement of both HE and employers in the moderation and development of the ASDAN Award Scheme, and in the development of 'communities of professional practitioners'.

Presentation of the Skills Portfolio approach used in training schemes for young school 'drop-outs' organised by the Integration Unit of the Aix-Marseille Education Authority

Joëlle Bruguière
Unit Head
Aix-Marseille Education Authority
Daet Education Office
Ministry of Education Integration Unit

I — The general context in which vocational certificates are awarded

- The structure of vocational certificates (CAP, BEP, Bac Pro, BTS) and test methods take account of:
  - the different groups concerned,
  - young people's different pathways,
  - their different experience.
- Vocational certification — i.e. the recognition and validation of skills acquired from training or occupational experience — is intended to meet the strong demand for validation by an official body.
- A certification standard, to be differentiated from the training curriculum, defines the expected level.
- The way in which certificates are awarded makes it possible to split up and take the tests in different ways.
- A global approach to skills gives meaning to each test as it is based on the mastery of technical, vocational and general knowledge and skills that can be put to use in different situations.

II — The educational approach of the Skills Portfolio for disadvantaged young people

II-1. Training schemes for very disadvantaged young people have two stages

Stage 1: Remotivation and construction of a career plan:
CIPPA (Cycles d'Insertion Professionnelle Par Alternance — Vocational integration by alternance courses)

Objectives:

To help young people *for whom a qualification seems impossible* to attend vocational training, either by entering apprenticeship or other vocational training schemes, or by returning to initial education, the ultimate objective being to make it possible for everyone to gain a level V qualification.

Target group:

Young people *aged 16 or more*, having problems at school and no plan, for whom a *transitional and pre-qualifying stage* is essential.

Validation:

For some young people on CIPPA courses: award of the CFG (Certificat de Formation Générale — General Training Certificate).

Educational methods and organisation of training schemes:

- individual treatment: skill review.
- personalised pathways.

- major emphasis on alternance: many professional partners.
- use of the 'Skills Portfolio' approach
- a supervisor for each young person.

Length of training:

Training varies from two to eight months depending on the length of time needed to construct a career plan.

- **Stage 2: Obtaining a vocational qualification:**
  Modular CAPs (Certificates of vocational aptitude)

Objectives:

To help *disadvantaged* young people, by appropriate methods and on the basis of their career plans, to gain an initial vocational certificate enabling them to enter the labour market on a better footing.

Target group:

Young people *aged 16 or more* who have completed CIPPA courses or final integration or special education school classes, *facing major problems at school* and wishing to prepare for a CAP at school.

Validation:

Validation by stages: credit units awarded after spot supervision.

Educational methods and organisation of training:

- individual treatment: skill review.
- use of the 'Skills Portfolio' approach.
- personalised pathways.
- high level of alternance.
- a supervisor for each young person.

Length of training:

Training varies from two to three years and depends on each young person's pathway and in particular validated units for each subject at the end of two years at school.

The third year is then worked out with the young person and professional partners: apprenticeship contracts (in most cases), qualification contracts or direct recruitment.

II-2. Definition of the Skills Portfolio

The Skills Portfolio is the concrete, practical and organised result of an approach that allows young people:

- to find out more about themselves,
- better to position themselves with respect to their social and occupational integration pathways by identifying what skills they already possess (knowledge, know-how and experience),
- better to manage their qualifying training pathways.

The approach used to formulate the Skills Portfolio is inductive:

- individual or group training,
- self-instruction,
- a permanent training dynamic.

The Skills Portfolio may include official validations of learning (all or part of certificates) and other attestations linked, for instance, to training schemes but which do not have the same standing as certificates.

It takes the form of a document (binder, open folder, etc.) in which the various skills that the person has acquired are recorded.

This is a resource for:

- **self-recognition** (since it enables self-evaluation),
- **recognition by others** (who are able to search for and find proof of stated skills),
- **institutional recognition** (since the portfolio contains certificates or parts of certificates or dispensations from tests given under the procedure for the validation of occupational experience).

The way in which the Skills Portfolio is put together may help to describe occupational activities and to pinpoint the skills arising from these so that an individual application dossier for the validation of occupational skills can then be completed.

III — Skills included in the portfolio

Skills may be listed as such as well as by the method by which they have been acquired, validated and/or recognised and the context in which they have been acquired, on the basis of:

1. Credit units awarded, i.e. skills forming part of the certification standards of vocational or technological certificates (vocational and general education streams) which are officially certified skills. These skills are regulated by law and validation methods are laid down in test regulations (assessment during training, spot testing, etc.).
2. Skills that 'go beyond' those contained in certification standards: acquired from school education, at training centres or in enterprise. These may include:
    - certain skills provided by occupational and personal experience;
    - skills students have acquired from activities outside or after school (taking part in a *mini-enterprise*, term of office as a *class representative*, responsibilities for *work in the community*, taking part in various *associations*, seasonal jobs, supervision of holiday camps, etc.).

Those skills that are not officially certified (validated) have to be recognised by a system of tests (attestations); these attestations are binding on their signatories but have no other value. Signatories must undertake that they have verified the existence of these skills.

IV — Skills Portfolio and validation or recognition of experience

The Skills Portfolio is therefore a resource that makes it possible to build on experience that has been validated (or certified) and experience that has simply been recognised.

V — Placing the Skills Portfolio on an operational footing

The Skills Portfolio, representing the outcome of a strategy, is a resource that serves the individual (student, apprentice, vocational training trainee, employee, self-employed worker, etc.):

- during school education,
- at the end of the review,
- looking for a first job,
- looking for a new job,

    or

- from the point of view of career management.

The Skills Portfolio is used in the Aix-Marseille Education Authority, in:

- vocational training at school (CAP, Bac Pro, BTS),
- the training schemes run by the Integration Unit,
- continuing training schemes.

This strategy, which expands the areas and places of evaluation, therefore acts as a guide for every young person throughout their initial and continuing training pathways: the approach is one of an educational progression: it supplements the certification system but is in no way an alternative to this system. It is specific to whoever owns it: the Skills Portfolio is designed to evolve and to be put together again whenever necessary by its author.

The integration of young people into active life

Jovens Inserção na vida activa (JIVA)

Maria Eugénia Santiago
Executive Coordinator of the Centro Social Paroquial Santo Antonio de Campolide

The reasons for this project

The crises of the 1970s, worsening living conditions, the globalisation of the economy, technological and scientific developments and economic growth without the creation of employment, have all increased social exclusion and poverty in Europe and the world.

Current situation

New poverty and new classes of poverty; labour market segmentation, insufficient integration of young people in the educational, training and employment systems.

Reactions

Studies on poverty by the World Bank and OECD, a drive for social and economic cohesion within the European Community, the White Papers on employment and education following on from the Maastricht Treaty.

An alternative approach

A new model of development — local integrated development and empowerment strategies.

Our experience

A local integrated development project in the poorest community of the region

The features characterising some areas of Campolide are low levels of self-esteem among young people and adults, deficient educational training, scholastic failure and high drop out levels, high rates of unemployment, drug abuse, alcoholism, etc. We are employing new strategies to develop the integration of the young people into society via education and training.

Aims:

- to promote integrated development in the community through the exercise of citizenship;
- to continue with training/overall integrated development of young people via occupational integration.

Project features:

- Open project.
- Flexible timetables adapted to the life styles of the target group (evenings, weekends and holidays).
- Participation of the young people throughout the length of the project — planning, resource identification, activities.

- Development of networked partnerships, networks of family, friends, neighbours and communities.
- Development of national and transnational partnerships.
- Promotion and diffusion of the native culture of such young people and their families.
- Promotion of multicultural integration, respect for young people and the managing conflicts via integrated solutions.
- Motivating young people to become reintegrated into educational and employment systems, to participate in the process as partners.

Conclusion

The aim of this project is to provide young people with the basic knowledge that can help them identify and appreciate their individual abilities in relation to their families and culture. Motivating them to acquire vocational and social skills. Integration of young people in the training/qualification system in order to acquire vocational skills and qualifications. Support of young people throughout the labour market integration process via training in proximity services that are to be set up.

Workshop 3

Objectives and methods of validation and certification?

Summary of the two sessions on 7 and 8 May

Angela Lambkin
FAS (IRL)
Clemens Romijn
ITS Universiteit van Nijmegen (NL)

A small group participated in a fruitful workshop. In spite of the time constraints everyone contributed and active discussion ensued.

Speaker 1, Dave Brockington (UK) spoke on the assessment function, and the results of a recent international study on assessment approaches and patterns.

Speaker 2, Marie Santiago (P) spoke of her experience on a project for seriously deprived young people in Lisbon and the issues which have been brought to her attention by this experience.

Speaker 3, Joëlle Bruguière (F) spoke of her experience in the Marseilles project and spoke of the use of Skills Portfolios to enable young people to better position themselves in the workplace.

Following this, all members shared some of their experiences and concerns about the assessment, validation and certification of excluded young people trying to integrate into the labour market.

Innovations and methods of best practice — points raised by group.

1. Partnerships:

    The involvement of the various partners mentioned are crucial in the effectiveness of these programmes. The best outcomes from the experiences of the group members included partnerships which included:

    - young persons e.g., contracts
    - between trainer and family
    - with local neighbourhood
    - with employers and trade unions.

2. Inclusion of formal and informal learning linked to pre-written standards of performance:

    The acknowledgement and recognition of all forms of learning, however it has been attained, was determined as best practice. These young people have failed in the formal system and often their informal learning is substantial and needs recognition. The recognition of this learning can only be done when it is linked to pre-written standards of performance in an accreditation of prior learning approach. Examples of systems in existence are:

    - record of achievement (UK)
    - skills portfolio (F)
    - new key skills programme (UK).

3. Reintegration of young people in to the mainstream a priority rather than certification:

    The successful reintegration of the young person from a position of disadvantage to an improved one was considered the objective of these programmes rather than the pursuit of adequate certification.

4. Personal active involvement of the individual in assessment process with focus on what he/she 'can do':
   Positive reinforcement of small successes is the best method of assessing these young people.

5. Best practice based on 'small steps' or unit-based assessment:
   - IRL
   - Netherlands.

   A number of systems of integrated assessment for this client group have been developed for this client group and deserve examination with a view to sharing the expertise developed.

6. Assessment, practically based; integrating theory and practice, activity based:
   Practical activity based assessment is more effective for this client group given low literacy and application levels.

7. Skills Portfolio a viable alternative (not used as a stand-alone assessment at present):
   Skills Portfolio an innovation which should be further explored as a viable means of continuously assessing these young people. At present it is not used as a stand-alone assessment but as part of a broader assessment (UK). The Skills Portfolio has also been introduced in Ireland for accreditation of prior learning in a number of sectors.

8. Flexibility of delivery of assessment:
   Flexibility of delivery is crucial to the effectiveness of assessment in this area. This ties in with overall flexibility of delivery of the programme itself — with evenings, Saturdays as well as flexible methodologies such as multimedia etc.

9. Access to assessments on EU-wide network:
   There are a number of assessment programs developed in the EU. A database of assessments on the Internet available EU-wide would be helpful.

10. Assessment design to involve teachers to optimise suitability:
    The partnership of teachers, trainers and developers of assessments is essential. Some experience of assessments developed in isolation from the teacher/trainer were noted and this was a concern.

11. Effective identification of training needs:
    Leads to higher standards (Black/Dylan, 1998 — London University).
    This was a final point of the group from a recent study on training needs.

Key issues to be addressed

Compatibility of mainstream structures and systems of assessment

The group recommended that the existing frameworks of assessment do not provide for the young person of disadvantage and this system needs to be extended to cater for their assessment requirements so that they are certified for skills and competencies acquired at their level.

Define clear linkages to national qualifications systems for access and transfer

In the experience of the group it is difficult for the young person coming from a special programme to access and transfer to mainstream programmes. In principle the system may allow transfer, but not in practice, because of competition for places, job prospects and other issues. The mainstream system needs to have clearly defined access and transfer for young people coming successfully from intervention type programmes.

Assessor competence and training

The group determined the need for assessor competence and training for the assessment of young disadvantaged people to be essential to effective testing. Special skills are needed to taken into account the disadvantage of the young person, to allow for variation in test methodology and delivery, and to assess the young person in the most positive manner.

Difficulty of assessing personal skills and their importance

Personal skills development is particularly important for disadvantaged young people to improve confidence, self esteem and communication skills as well as decision-making, teamwork and others. The measurement of personal skill attainment is not easy — some organisations have methodologies. Personal skills need to be focused on for further assessment development.

Design of suitable assessments for this client group

Reflections of the group included a concern for good 'design of assessments' to suit the needs of the disadvantaged young person. The low level of achievement, the problems of the young person suggest that the assessments should be of a special nature. Similar to the point above, the assessment should be designed in a simple format integrating the skills and knowledge using a practically based task. These tasks could be built into a modular structure and use a formal continuous assessment methodology.

Improve level of recognition

Concerns were raised as to the recognition by employers, educators of the certification and training undertaken by these young people. Greater promotion of the programmes and their outcomes is recommended.

Put certification higher on the agenda

In the view of the group, certification deserves a higher level of attention. Without formal evidence of attainment the young person stands to gain very little in an already difficult environment.

Workshop 4

How should trainers operate and what professional skills should they have? (Teaching teams, tutoring and mentoring, training of trainers)

The training of tutors for social cooperatives forming part of vocational training and work induction projects for disadvantaged young people

Alain Goussot
Centro studi analisi di psicologia e sociologia applicate (CSAPSA) (I)

This project is one of the real-situation training projects (vocational training for young people with handicaps or learning difficulties linked to social or cultural disadvantages) planned by the Emilia Romagna region in particular in the Province of Bologna. These training projects which integrate training, school and enterprise are being developed by setting up an integrated system that brings together a variety of partners, resources and skills: teachers, enterprise tutors, educators and local social service workers. The training model is one of training in a real working situation where students can find out about their potential and learn by working. The approach is one of providing a network of support for a social integration project through which students can gain vocational skills and social autonomy. The trainers and researchers involved in formulating these integration projects and putting them into practice have become aware that it is important to provide tutors (workers responsible for supervising young people in enterprise and for passing on the necessary occupational skills) with training in and a better awareness of the problems raised by the fight against social exclusion as well as in educational models and practices making it possible to manage diversity from the point of view of integration. In our region in particular, where the economic and social fabric is made up of cooperatives and small and medium-sized enterprises, the cooperative sector plays a key role in training and integration projects for people who are socially disadvantaged. Under law, it is possible to set up integrated social production cooperatives, at least 35 % of whose employees are people considered to be socially disadvantaged (disabled, drop-outs, young people with histories of social delinquency, young immigrants, travellers and refugees). These enterprises help to integrate young people excluded from other training circuits and promote the creation of concrete job opportunities: the sectors of activity in which this integration training is taking place include the environment, public spaces, agritourism, crafts, small metal-working enterprises, agriculture, stock breeding and some areas of the service sector. It is important in this context to provide enterprise tutors with training in educational and teaching methods through which the integration process can be managed.

Target group

Enterprise workers acting as tutors and instructors for workplace integration and experience periods. Integrated social cooperative workers: this year, for instance, 20 or so workers from varying economic backgrounds in the Emilia Romagna region are managing the retraining and integration of various groups of disadvantaged young people.

Content of the training scheme

Training for tutors is divided into three teaching areas:

(1) The problems raised by the fight against social exclusion and by integration:
tutors work with specialists on the topics of disability, marginalisation and social delinquency and on the topic of diversity. These topics are approached from a social and psycho-educational point of view.

(2) Methods of work integration within vocational training:
The various stages of project construction and achievement: comment on and reading and analysis of the needs of the enterprise — trainee system; ways in which projects can be run in practice and how the various partners can take part; group and individual evaluation; approaches to teaching methods for autonomy and integration; mediation work: mediation as a way of managing the educational process

is a key aspect of the integration process; integration as an objective and working method; the importance of (formal and informal) links with local networks in order to support and assist those in the most difficult and problematic situations.

(3) The role of enterprise and in particular of social cooperatives in the integration process:
Italian legislation on the work integration of people at risk of social exclusion, the laws on social cooperatives, agreements between the Ministry of Labour and the 'third sector'; the important part played by enterprises with social aims in the fight against exclusion and the importance of targeted vocational training pathways.

The method used is one of interactive education and on-going group discussion work that takes the technical and professional experience accumulated by these worker-tutors as a starting point.

Teacher training. Why?

Miriam Díez Piñol
COPSA S.L.
Antonia Ferrer Torres
Coordinators: Carme Turull Bassomba
Patricia Sagrera Rosquelles

From our experience in the area of education and social services, we have been able to corroborate that activities linked to these services are experiencing difficulties. Social and family structural changes, a lack of psycho-educational materials and a lack of credibility in the educator's role, imply extra efforts on their part. Such effort is unproductive most of the time. The continuing of this situation causes serious problems for education professionals as well as for adolescents and their families.

Taking these factors into account, the COPSA Training School has been working since 1987 to provide education professionals with a pedagogical environment that favours diversity in educational and learning methods, adapted both to the current and individual needs of young people and their families.

In this document, we will explain some of the factors that we consider important in order to understand the current crisis experienced by the professional educator. We will also analyse some of the trials and results obtained through training teachers over the years.

Introduction

Is it possible to precisely determine the educational responsibilities of teachers? How and why are such functions allocated to them, functions that that have nothing to do with mere instructing or transmitting theoretical or practical knowledge? Without doubt, we find ourselves faced with one of the main problems in today's educational system. An educational role is implicitly demanded of the teacher and it is one for which he or she has never been prepared. We concur with Noddins in that *'the traditional organisation of the school is unsuitable for contemporary society, both intellectually and morally'* (Gordillo, 1996). This situation generates feelings of uselessness and personal insecurity in the teacher. The discomfort affects their personal health and increases the rate of illnesses. In Spain it is estimated that more than 50 % of teaching staff are made up by temporary floating members.

Such discomfort is not confined to the Spanish educational scene. As a rule, structural social and family changes affect the whole range of educational models. As long as this situation continues, the credibility of the school and its employees as people responsible for the training and education of young people, will decrease.

Factors which explain the crisis in the educational role of the teacher

Frequently, teachers are upset and depressed because of not knowing how to solve problems which arise within the classroom and outside it. As we stated, more than 50 % of the staff in some centres are made up by temporary members. This means that there are very high rates of illness. According to official data, the educational sector has the highest occupational sickness rates. Much of this is psychosomatic ailments (migraine, 'flu, depression, burn-out) and tends to be linked to anxiety and stress.

We wish to get away from simplistic explanations of why this situation exists. There have been a variety of factors and variables that have directly affected the educational system:

- Reforms in educational systems: This has meant a series of changes and transformations in educational centres in order to adapt them to new legislation.
- Structural social and family change: Over the past few years changes have taken place requiring a redefinition of the objectives and functions allocated to the school. Changes which include, among others, the increase in single-parent families, the breakdown of the traditional family structure and the large-scale entry of women into the job market.

In this sense, the school is entrusted not only with the transmission of theoretical and practical knowledge, but also with aspects such as developing study habits, acquiring skills for problem solving, counselling and providing advice for teenagers and their families, for emotional development, etc.

In the past few years, it has been shown that families in general have serious difficulties in providing their children with educational and behavioural standards. At the same time, this educational role has been assigned to the school. However, the professionals in the educational sector have not been taught the psycho- educational strategies required to provide these functions that families expect of them. At the same time, professionals see themselves as being incapable of guiding families, on instructing how to transmit social values and educational standards to their children.

- Technological change: Technological innovation, at a general level, has affected educational centres in a particular way. The introduction of computers and multimedia into the classroom has led to new stresses being placed on teachers. Because of their lack of training and adjustment to such technological change, teachers have been unable to provide young people with appropriate educational standards.
- Changes in the role of the teacher: At present, the teacher is required to provide more than a mere transmission of knowledge to pupils. The teacher has to be capable of giving appropriate answers to behavioural problems that arise with young people. They also have to face difficulties deriving from the social and technological changes outlined earlier. The youth of today receives, as a rule, much greater stimuli than that of previous generations. At the same time, such stimuli are immensely more varied. It is important that such 'over-stimulation' be channelled correctly. To do this a certain amount of training and adjustment time is required. At present, we are only just learning of the positive and negative repercussions that the information technology boom is having on minors at social, cognitive and health level. Some of the elements under study are the effects of television, the Internet and computers. From results obtained to date, we can say that there has been a quantitative increase in participative activities and games. However, teachers still have insufficient levels of preparation to be able to handle and provide educational answers to both the positive and negative effects that such new pedagogical tools have.

These are the factors broadly affecting the current situation of education professionals. In general, they were never prepared during their initial training to face the problems which are found during the actual practice of their profession. This has been marked by '*decontextualised theory and limited practice with a lack of direction*' (De Millán, 1986). Their qualifications have been mainly centred on instruction. For this reason, they have important gaps when it comes to providing a social/family function. At the outset of their professional careers, teachers find that they are obliged 'to improvise' answers to the problems that arise. A second factor is the intense social pressure under which trainers carry out their profession. The teacher is forced to prepare young people in order for them to gain access to a qualified job. Education has come under pressure and gained further responsibilities due to the shortage of jobs.

In conclusion, we are convinced that the current situation of teachers can be improved. This means providing them with new educational perspectives on which to base their practices. It is becoming more and more important for teachers to be able to rely on permanent guidance and retraining in psycho-educational matters. In this sense, the Educators' School Programme is oriented both towards training and the development of the teachers themselves. In general terms, the programme covers the following aspects:

(a) Overcoming the psycho-educational gaps that exist in both novice and experienced teachers.
(b) Making teachers aware that they should be responsible for their students results. As T. Popkewitz (1977) points out, 'the meaning of ideas is decisively influenced both by the social context in which they are produced as well as the strategies used in their teaching'.
(c) Ensuring that the training activities carried out with young people have a firm educational basis.

The current situation of the professional in the educational and social services

In our experience in the area of teacher training we have been able to learn how professionals experience this situation, when finding themselves subjected to important educational and social pressure:

*   On one hand, there is an over saturation of training in purely instructive matters. However, what professionals lack is training in the psycho-educational strategies that allow them to handle problems of a behavioural nature and attitudes when dealing with minors and young people.
*   On the other hand, there is a lack of knowledge of the educational responsibilities that teachers have towards minors and young people. According to our results, we have found a lack of coordination between actions being carried out in schools and those within the family itself. This lack of communication between them hinders the solving of many problems that young people have. In many cases, it is an aggravating factor in young people's behavioural problems.

Alternative models to the present situation. The COPSA Training School Programme

Taking into account all the factors covered in previous points, we consider it important to provide teachers with the necessary psycho-educational standards and tools, so that they will be able:

*   to differentiate between educating, training and instructing;
*   to evaluate the individual needs of each pupil and be able to provide them with an appropriate educational response;
*   to adapt the curriculum and the educational project where necessary;
*   to adopt a greater variety of educational methodologies;
*   to direct normal development according to the evolutionary stage of the students (analysis, observation, evaluation and diagnosis);
*   to guide and advise the family;
*   to vary the means of intervention according to the needs of the individual;
*   to propose educational periods having variable timing, according to the needs of each person;
*   to choose those activities and didactic materials that favour active education;
*   to promote confidence and motivation in the minors and young people;
*   to propose activities that take into account the different educational objectives foreseen by each person.

In order to do this, we have put forward a teacher training programme that has two important components:

*   The first is an advising function for teachers and professionals in education in general. The problems and/or situations that students bring to teachers require effective and rapid educational answers. Using answers based on trial and error or on 'improvisation', as commented earlier, may increase problems and generate unsuitable behaviour in young people.
*   The second component of the training programme that we have drawn up is based on a collaboration between the family and the school. We have demonstrated that the more the various parties involved in the education of young people collaborate, the better the academic results and the more the social and personal integration both inside and outside the school improves.

This programme has been applied in both State and private centres: compulsory teaching, vocational training and special educational needs centres. The results of the programme can be observed in the very first month of its application. These results are produced in different areas:

(a) In relation to the institutional/social context:

- Training of the educational professionals in psycho-educational material. This training guides the professional on how to assist the minor or young person in developing in a way that is integrated with and suited to his environment.
- Educational coherency, i.e., the correlation between educational processes themselves and the needs of the young people.
- Advice to the teacher on integrating young people in the school, home and social environments.
- Preparation of the teacher in guiding the personality development of young people during their adolescence. This favours the subsequent integration of the young person into the working world.
- The acquisition of knowledge by the teacher in order to develop aspects related to students' motivation, attitudes and values.

(b) In relation to the personal development of young people:

- improvement in the social adjustment of young people;
- improvements in interpersonal relationships and social skills;
- reduction of aggressiveness (inside and outside the classroom/collective);
- improvement in self-esteem and the sense of security of young people;
- integration, adjustment and motivation of young people in those activities that they are carrying out and towards their environment;
- reduction in truancy and an improvement in school performance;
- greater involvement of the young in the training and job placement process;
- prevention of addictive behaviour;
- reduction in sexually transmitted diseases;
- prevention of early pregnancies.

(c) In relation to the family and community:

- changes in the educational behaviour of progenitors in relation to different areas of growing up: intellect, health, etc.;
- greater participation of the family in the school and in the community.

Conclusions

One means of combating scholastic failure at school and favouring the social and occupational integration of young people is to improve the psycho-educational conditions of the professionals in charge of them. In this way, teachers will be better able to provide educational answers suited to young people at social risk, by detecting their difficulties, helping with their transition to the training and/or work system.

The better this educational task is coordinated with the functions carried out by the family and institutions in the community, the greater will be the success of the educative actions carried out by teachers.

Bibliography

Gordillo M. (1996), *Orientación y comunidad. La responsabilidad social de la orientación,* Madrid, Alianza Universidad.

Ángel San Martín Alonso (1986), *El pensamiento pedagógico en el profesor,* in *Revista de Psicología y Pedagogía* (1986), pp. 24-32.

Popkewitz T. (1977), *Los valores latentes del curriculum centrado en las disciplinas,* in Gimeno, Sacristán y Pérez Gómez (1983), *La enseñanza: su teoría y su práctica,* Madrid, Editorial Akal.

Workshop 4

How should trainers operate and what professional skills should they have?

Summary of the two sessions on this topic on 7 and 8 May

Paul Forbes
Leeds Second Chance School (UK)
Ulrike Wisser
BBJ Servis (D)

Introduction

The workshop received some interesting presentations from Spain and Italy, following which a participative and informative discussion ensued. This is a summary of the key events and it is clear that there are common themes running through the various workshop presentations.

The Workshop response

All of us know that the world of education/training is changing rapidly. The conference heard that 10 years from now 80 % of the technology used today will be obsolete. The level of skills, knowledge and understanding necessary to secure and sustain employment is increasing. Just as the nature of work and the changes in local, national and global markets are placing new demands on employees.

Business must retain its competitive edge and in seeking to do so its greatest asset is its workforce. Investing in people will lead to reduced errors in service/production, the delivery of quality products and services and higher levels of overall customer satisfaction.

Potential employees wanting to enter the world of work must display high levels of behavioural competence. They must be literate and numerate, able to work in a team, problem solve, and possess good communication skills.

Changes in technology means that students increasingly can exercise greater choice about where and when they learn and the way in which they learn. Education and training providers can offer courses from a whole range of centres and sites. Employers often require training that meets their very specific needs and through the Internet and CD-ROMS students now have access to a substantial range of education/training provision.

The range of skills teachers/trainers must have are significant and it is too time-consuming to list them all, but the following gives a flavour:

Assessment skills; feedback skills; coaching skills; counselling skills; effective teamwork skills; mentoring skills; marketing skills; communication skills; information technology skills; guidance skills.

Teachers must be able to devise new training responses, to assess competence, to evaluate training and to interact with a range of students all of whom may have very differing needs.

The Workshop expressed concern that many of the education/training responses fail to take account of the needs of those young people deemed to be disaffected and often socially excluded. The whole structure of the education/training response throughout Europe was inappropriate. The institutionalised process that students are subjected to often turns them off learning. Students should drive the process rather than have to conform to it. The Workshop felt that the key reasons as to why people dropped out of education/training were not fully understood and there was a need to obtain more information on this very important issue. Could education/training providers respond in a more flexible way?

There was a general feeling that attempts to reintegrate young people who had dropped out of the learning process often came too late on. Secondary education was far too late, the intervention needed to be much earlier.

The school and the community were inextricably linked and teachers/trainers needed to recognise and include the pupil/student learning experiences outside of school. These needed to be accredited and turned to the pupils' advantage by linking them to national vocational qualifications. The education/training centres and the pupils are part of the wider social community.

Spain and Italy

The inputs into the Workshop from Spain and Italy highlighted the need for teachers to be skilled in transmitting knowledge, capable of developing effective working relationships with pupils/students, and able to access staff development/training programmes which develop their own learning. The Workshop also referred to the need to train supervisors in the private sector in ways of working with those young people who may not immediately demonstrate an acceptable level of skills and competence. The value of experiential learning could not be understated. Disaffected young people needed support/workers/mentors to help them integrate into the world of work and to encourage them back into learning.

The contribution from trade unions and community organisations in helping young people back into work thereby enabling them to become members of an inclusive society were also important. These contributions needed to be recognised.

Finally, teachers needed to be valued. They could not be held responsible for all the ills of society. In Spain 50 % of the teaching profession were on temporary contracts. Other professionals need to support the learning process and more stability must be brought back into the education/training sector. Teachers need to update their skills to enable them to respond to the ever-changing needs of employers and young people. They will after all be subject to continuous review and development and will play a leading role in taking us forward into the next century.

Toward European networks

The first round was used by the participants for discussing the potential of the different specialities of a European network:

- What are the very important contents and questions, for which the European level could serve as a think-tank?
- To which problems European involvement or competence brings an added-value effect?
- Due to which detailed questions and segments are innovative measures needed where is innovation at transnational level feasible?
- Related to methods of cooperation the question was formulated as: cooperation has to be organised in an effective and continuous way, what kind of methods could lead to such a structure?

Joint projects are interesting to aspects where similar problems and common solutions exist and where strengthening of similarity is positive in the sense of solution-finding. Transfer of best practise and know-how is an important form of exchange; the form of exchange should be in correlation with content and objectives.

Referring to the document 'Accomplishing Europe through Education & Training' of the Study Group on Education & Training, special propositions were repeated and evaluated as necessary due to the workshop-topic:

- develop initial and continuing teacher education and training by the identification and discovery of best practice;
- institute a specific programme of exchanges and in-service education and training for head teachers and directors of education and training establishments;
- encourage innovative learning practices in educational establishments;
- pinpoint, study and disseminate good practice with respect to productivity and the search for quality in educational establishments and training centres;
- devise common methods for the evaluation of education and training based on experiences at national levels, in order to benefit from a comparative dimension.

Contents of European network activities as common questions:

1. Strengthening the teachers and educator's capacities to prevent dropouts at the first stage. Everybody in the workshop was conscious on the divided responsibilities between Member States and European Union on school, but stressed the need of looking for new approaches to prevent school failure. Identifying best practises in the training of teachers and educators.

2. Enlarging the partnership of actors responsible for training of trainers, teachers, educators and social workers; new cooperations are needed in the field of public authorities and administrations, mainly where responsible for universities, training, school education and vocational further education.

3. The contents of enlarged and new cooperations should ensure a wider range of professional skills for all involved in training and teaching, qualifications in self-employment, working and acting culture in enterprises, key-qualifications, etc., more professional professors.

4. Development of a profile of a trainer, who is able to cope with rapidly changing problems of the youngster, changing occupations and technical skills and variable needs of guidance.

5. Including the family as a competent and regular partner in the education of disadvantaged young persons, the family should be a part of the training and education team and to be qualified and enabled to take over these tasks.

European networking should be based on two principles, as asked for by the participants, flexibility and continuity.

Summarised by one member of the workshop, a function of the European level in intensifying their efforts of preventing dropout and failure could be:

- development of a mentoring programme for trainers, who's task is to guide socially excluded,
- to initiate resources,
- to promote new concepts of training of mentors,
- to support mutual recognition.

Workshop 5

Participation of the company in training
(objectives and arrangements)

Experiences from the 'Qualified Helpers' scheme in Linz

Aloïs Reischl
Berufsschule Linz

This information is based upon the project-management of the 'Countdown' project which is equally concerned with this theme.

1. Introduction

Unemployment, continual restructuring of industries, part-time employment and other factors are among the reasons why young people fail to find jobs and succeed in education.

All countries are seeking to provide better prospects for young people. In Upper Austria many efforts are being made to find acceptable solutions. One of these is a training course for unskilled young people with the aim of increasing their chances of employment.

Normally in Austria young people who wish to immediately leave elementary school conclude an apprenticeship training agreement with a company authorised to train apprentices and they are then required to attend vocational schools. This type of vocational education is known as the dual vocational training system (Dual) since the training has twin components: the company and the apprentices' part-time vocational school.

Young people who cannot find a company to take them on in the Dual system but who still wish to work and study can now enrol in other in other projects. One of these is 'Countdown', another for girls is known as 'Magma'.

This kind of training course started in Upper Austria in 1997. The reason for the projects was an increasing number of unskilled and unemployed young people. Such young people suffer both from the difficult situation in the labour market and from the consequences of Austrian youth protection legislation which strictly controls working hours and recreation time.

For this latter reason, companies don't wish to employ unskilled young people under the age of 18. The 'Countdown' project should help improve the chances of participants entering the labour market in two ways:

- First, beneficiaries will gain basic qualifications in different vocational sectors. Above all it is necessary for the young people to get into the vocational school in time, and if they are fortunate, to get an apprenticeship place.
- Second, many the participants will be aged over 18 by the end of the training and will no longer be affected by Austrian youth protection legislation.

2. Financing of the project

This project is 80 % subsidised by the regional labour office (AMS) and 20 % by regional government. The government also finances the cost of the vocational schools.

During the entire training period the beneficiaries are employed by the Austrian labour market service and have full insurance cover. The participants receive around ATS 3 500 each month. Apprentices in their first year receive a similar amount, but paid by the company they work for.

3. Target group

The beneficiaries range from 15 to 19 years of age and have left school without the necessary qualifications to obtain an apprenticeship.

In general they have poor intellectual and educational levels and are often socially disadvantaged. Either they have been unemployed for at least four months or they have been endorsed by previous training courses (also subsidised by the regional labour office).

4. Aims of the training

The aim is to increase the employment chances of young people. The Austrian labour market service demands that around 50 % of beneficiaries become employed at the end of the training.

The beneficiaries gain basic vocational and social qualifications and increase their ability to live an independent and responsible lifestyle. They get practical training according to their abilities and interests and in accordance with the demands of the labour market.

Beneficiaries with higher levels of education equally have the chance of attending vocational schools. If some of them wish to go on to an apprenticeship after training they start vocational school in the second class. Of course it is necessary to obtain positive results, therefore an essential part of the project concerns the training structure.

5. Structure of the training

Beneficiaries are assigned by the Austrian labour market service.

Young people who haven't attended previous courses pass through a diagnosis phase of about three weeks. Diagnosis includes a medical check-up, psychological tests, commercial ability tests and craftsmanship tests.

After diagnosis, new groups are formed and preparation is carried out. The beneficiaries then start their practical in-company training. Adequate work places for on-the-job training have to be found by the staff of trainers.

The young people work three days per week in-company, the remaining two days they receive training at vocational school in a special class and in their project group. Here they are given the chance to improve their knowledge of German, maths, and get basic computer training.

Training agreements with companies are made for six months. Once a week trainers contact the firms and collect information about the behaviour and performance of the beneficiaries during work.

One principal function of the training staff is to balance the interests of the beneficiaries and the companies. At the end of six months in-company practical work the trainers assess if there is a real chance of the trainee becoming employed there. If there is no possibility the training staff has to then change company. In cases where the trainee takes up employment the trainee leaves the training course.

At the moment we are running three groups
- retail sales (Linz)
- gastronomy catering (Altmünster)
- craftsmanship courses (Steyr).

The instruction-units (IU) total 560 and are spread over the following subjects:

- political instruction 40 IU
- German & communications 40 IU
- occupational English 40 IU
- commercial instruction 120 IU
- special instruction 320 IU.

Religious instruction and physical education is voluntary.

Special instruction is divided into retail sales, gastronomy catering and craftsmanship courses.

Part-time vocational school training is organised as follows:

- retail sales group at Linz, two days a week for one semester
- gastronomy catering at Altmünster, eight weeks continuous (trainees are provided with accommodation)
- craftsmanship courses at Steyr, eight weeks continuous (trainees are provided with accommodation).

In addition, for three hours a week the beneficiaries receive specialised vocational training in either catering, the building trade or commerce via their project group.

At the vocational school this group is taught by specialist teachers. At project level six trainers handle 50 beneficiaries. Each trainer is responsible for 8-9 participants of the group. Training staff advise the beneficiaries, discuss their problems and remain in contact with their parents. The contact person for the school is the project manager. The trainers also seek out the training work places and monitor the adolescents and company tutors during the on the job training. In the case of any problems they intervene.

Enterprise participation in training

Marie-Jo Sanchez
Centre d'Education et Formation en Alternance (CEFA) (B)

I. Introduction

Two key social issues have played a part in the development of socio-occupational integration in Belgium: youth unemployment, which has in the past been explained by young people's under-qualification, and dropping out from school.

Alternative training seems to be a useful solution to both problems. Various alternative training formulae have been set up, first in the association sector and then in education.

The notion of part-time compulsory education was introduced by law in 1983: between the ages of 15 and 18, young people can attend part-time compulsory education that can be supplemented by part-time vocational apprenticeship in enterprise.

The *Centres d'Enseignement à Horaire Réduit* (CEHR) — (Part-time Education Centres), renamed the *Centres d'Education et de Formation en Alternance* (CEFA) — (Alternative Education and Training Centres) in 1991, were set up to provide an alternance training structure for this part-time compulsory education. At the same time, starting in the Brussels region, non-profit-making integration associations became recognised operators and were subsidised by the public authorities responsible for employment and training.

In parallel, the public authorities began a process, still continuing today, of offering incentives to enterprises to encourage them to become involved in these socio-occupational integration pathways and in particular to offer new employment.

The sectors participate to a varying extent in this construction that tries to combine socio-occupational integration with job creation.

A number of questions are being raised today about the relevance and efficiency of this system, especially as regards the participation of enterprise in training:

1. In Belgium, enterprise participation in training is less the outcome of thinking about vocational training methods than an attempt to meet a need to create jobs.
2. Alternative training in Belgium is designed by associations and not by the education sector. It has never really become a resource through which vocational training can be transformed.
3. While the economic world has been a key partner from the outset, enterprises do not seem to have played a genuine part in constructing the concept of alternance training.
4. The public authorities have been the main players in socio-occupational integration, each level of political power formulating its own concepts and generating specific implementation formulae.

In these circumstances, it would seem that there is a real need to impose consistency on the various resources currently in existence.

This situation makes us think that the vocational training system has reached a point where it has to go beyond two basic contradictions:

- Perceiving vocational training as a tool for resolving social problems places the economic sector in a position where it has to take a 'civic' responsibility that goes well beyond the sphere of training.
- The economic world cannot be associated with the development of vocational training solely from a job creation point of view.

On the contrary, enterprises must also be involved with the educational concept in the strict sense, albeit without denying them their key position as holders of future employment.

These two contradictions are the stumbling block that needs to be overcome if enterprises are to be able to take a position in the debate and to take account of the particular group that is the focus of the debate.

II. Areas for thought

While we have managed to achieve a relatively structured regulatory framework in Belgium, it seems that we are lagging behind as regards the formulation of genuine policies of socio-occupational integration.

Our attempt to set up a second chance school project is underpinned in this respect by our concern to impose institutional consistency on the schemes put forward as part of the education process overall.

This means firstly that responsibilities need to be distributed to all the partners involved in integration in a way that is in keeping with their skills.

This also means that an educational plan, which gives a central position to the target group for which it is intended and which takes account of the social and cultural characteristics of this group, needs to be drawn up.

- Enterprise is perceived as a full partner in a training pathway that is intended to integrate young people into social as well as economic life and to develop their 'civic' responsibility and which is therefore defined as participation in an educational process irrespective of a certain outcome in enterprise itself. Enterprise is perceived as a tool for learning about society in the same way as a training centre.
- The tutoring function in this case acquires a training and educational dimension that goes beyond the currently accepted dimension of the learning of technical skills.
  The tutor is the person who will enable young people to discover and to take their place in active life. Providing tutors with training in teaching methods is a fundamental concern of our project.
- From this point of view, the training centre then becomes a steering and supervising structure for young people; it therefore becomes the basic tool that young people can use.

Enterprises and training centres are therefore the tools on which the second chance school is based. They are the places and resources that enable young people to construct a life plan through their ability to make choices from the real context of social life in general.

In this process, the progression is from a situation of possible options open to young people to a situation in which these young people ask to participate in an occupational and social context.

By way of conclusion, our reply to the topic being discussed at this workshop on enterprise participation in training is therefore chiefly to advocate enterprises not just as external and necessary partners but as active partners in a global and necessary educational process.

We have looked briefly at the Belgian context surrounding this partnership with enterprise for training for disadvantaged young people.

While support from the economic world is not particularly forthcoming in this respect, this 'failing' could in the long term be turned into an advantage; that of civic responsibility.

If the threat of inevitable unemployment for young people is a factor of social imbalance and if non-employment is a structural fact that requires responses connected with a global redefinition of work and employment, the education of coming generations must, therefore, take the form of learning in a real context.

When perceived in this way, we can move away from an approach which focuses on people because they are excluded and start looking in detail at how our society can take educational and collective responsibility for all its young people.

Company participation in training

Roberto Serra (SOLCO) (I)

I believe that it will become more and more important to reflect on the possible role that a company or employer can play in regard to education and training. This is a fairly recent discussion and there is as yet little literature dealing with it. The explanation up until now is perhaps that the word 'enterprise' or 'company' is only associated with concepts in the world of economics, profits and market forces.

In an entrepreneurial environment, education and training has mainly focused, and still focuses, for the most part on technical aspects, aiming to increase production or recruit specific candidates.

It is only in a few cases that companies put efforts into education and training, develop training schemes, carry out projects relating to education and training, and make them an integral part of company life. I believe, given the theme of this conference, that young people are victims of a lack of effort at company level. A company that does not invest in training (since people are the real resources of the company), tends inevitably to wither. It cuts certain social ties, particularly with schools, and ends up with a one-way-market approach. In short, it cannot renovate or revitalise itself because it does not engage in the development of educational technology and it does not consider new ways of reflecting on its own role and mission.

In Italy, this problem is particularly widespread. For example, many companies, in the past two or three years, have found it difficult to fill positions in which young and well-qualified people are required. It seems that no one, either schools or other institutions (and in particular employers and companies), bothered to invest in training, particularly for young people. The result is that many young people who for various reasons did not attend or complete university, are equally excluded from entry into the labour market.

At this point, the following question arises: What does providing training to young people by an employer or company mean exactly?

I work for an organisation known as SOL.CO. (Solidarity and Cooperation). It is a union of social cooperatives, or put another way, a union of companies which aim to combine two aspects that are normally considered incompatible: entrepreneurship and solidarity towards those who are excluded and disadvantaged. SOL.CO is a cooperative; it provides and sells services in the social and economic welfare fields, it produces training programs for its own cooperatives, but also for other schools and public organisations. In Italy, this kind of organisation is particularly prevalent, in the north they have been steadily growing over the past 10 years.

It might be useful to summarise some aspects of my own experience as both a social entrepreneur and trainer:

- First, the low age at which people enter social enterprises: The average age of managers and directors is around 30 and, in many cases even less. This figure falls even further if you look at the operators of cooperatives who, in the majority of cases, are also members of the enterprise. In short, they have made an entrepreneurial choice.
- We have tried to provide explanations of this phenomena: Young people, beyond their cultural and educational levels, when given concrete opportunities, prove to be particularly interested in social and solidarity questions that involve other young people similar to them. I should like to remind you that our cooperatives also undertake the rehabilitation of drug-addicts, of mentally ill young people, of chil-

dren and adolescents who have been abandoned or who are in distressed situations, of ex-prisoners or convicted persons required to carry out community service.

- It therefore seems that the so-called 'social enterprise', merely by the fact that it is a company and that it has a social nature, has an attraction for young people who would otherwise remain inactive and not realise their potential.

When the company, or the social enterprise, undertakes the training process, it is necessary to have clear objectives and to consider methodological aspects:

- First, links with schools: In our experience, there are many opportunities for collaboration with schools at different levels. For example at lower and higher secondary level we organise meetings with parents about the problems of growing up, of adolescence, of delinquency, about studying and working, and how to guide young people in their choices once they have left compulsory education at 14.
- Second, links with public administrations in order to work with them and organise initiatives and activities directed at preventing delinquency.
- Third, the necessity of a social enterprise being rooted in its own community.
- Fourth, the importance of spreading knowledge within the community of laws that help the young people in various ways. In Italy, in the entrepreneurial field, we have, for example, Law 44/86. This legislation provides facilities and funding to companies set up by young people aged between 18 and 35; they can establish agricultural enterprises, handicrafts, industries or service companies. This law also has a formative nature because it requires that young people produce a real business plan, with a complete market analysis, strategic choices, operational choices, marketing and financial plans. This means that they must prepare themselves extremely well. Finally, the legislation makes available funds for entrepreneurial training that the young people can request. Another interesting law is the one which created 'Informagiovani' (Inform young people). These are services managed by public administrations or along with social cooperatives, and their aim is to inform young people about all kinds of employment opportunities. A young person can go to one of these centres and consult a database providing information on the different employment possibilities, the required qualifications, courses and training and they can request further information from the staff which normally is made up by young people. Today, Informagiovani centres exist all over the country and they are of great assistance at educational and vocational level in guiding young people.
- Another important aspect relates to our social cooperation role: much of the requested training relates to 'self- advancement' training. In 'self-advancement' training young people not only become familiar with the entrepreneurial skills and techniques, but, from a formative point of view, are given assistance in promoting themselves, better understanding their own abilities and how best to use them, combining creativity and pragmatism. In Italy, school education very often does not deal with such subjects, it does not encourage initiative and it is not always formative. I don't believe that the many young people who drop out of the education system should be considered to have failed. It is necessary to create other possibilities for growth and learning for such young people.
- At the level of training methodologies, we use so-called 'active' methods. This means that we do not offer didactic or one-dimensional single methods, where the teacher transmits and the audience passively listens. While there is nothing wrong with this, it must be combined with training techniques which actively involve the students and which makes them express themselves and become aware of their own expectations; which lets them get used to working with others and acting as members of a team, enabling them to recognise and increase leadership abilities, enabling them to use their creativity.

This kind of approach functions particularly well with young people because it puts them at the centre of the learning process.

In Italy a lot of young people drop out from university. I believe that one possible explanation may be found in the inappropriate and impersonal teaching methodology that keeps young people at a distance rather than getting closer to them.

The ways in which to fight social exclusion, and above all the exclusion of young people may be numerous. But the more paths there are, the more people working in this direction will be required. Educating and assisting young people is not merely a family or a school task, it also applies to other areas, such as the entrepreneurial environment.

We must all look at the population of young people from an educational point of view, this means investing in the future human resources of our society.

We are trying to provide teaching rules and social goals because both are written into the charter of our cooperatives and because we believe in the learning society and in the teaching and educational community.

Workshop 5

Enterprise participation in training

Summary of the two days' sessions on this topic

Eneko Astigarraga, Prospektiker and
Joseba Egia, 'Lan Ekintza' Local Development Agency, Bilbao (E)
Jean-Claude Bourcel
Second Chance School, Marseilles (F)

Experiences

The workshop offered us an opportunity to find out about various experiences in the area of enterprise participation in training:

- an Austrian experience: AMS presented by Aloïs Reischl;
- a Belgian experience: the CEFA presented by Marie-Jo Sanchez;
- an Italian experience: the case of Brescia presented by Roberto Serra.

Our discussion also took account of French, Irish and Portuguese experiences presented by training agencies rather than enterprises.

Enterprises can clearly participate in the qualification and occupational integration of young people in different ways (dual training, alternative training, second chance schools, apprenticeship projects, etc.).

There is, however, a common problem in all cases:

- the need for enterprises to play their part in educational thinking and young people's educational projects,
- the need for enterprises to play their part in the evaluation and validation of young people's training and qualifications.

The risks and problems include:

- the problem of finding apprenticeship places for young people;
- the risk of giving priority to short-term integration projects which consequently neglect the long term;
- the fact that enterprises are in some cases interested only in financial aid and are not genuinely willing to offer training;
- often, that enterprises feel that they are being over-used by training agencies and schools. There is a real risk that enterprises will be saturated by the existing training system.

The key questions raised by the debate

- Enterprises need to play more of a part in the training process at a very early stage from the outset of training, even from the point of view of teaching methods and integration which is still rather underdeveloped.
- It has to be stressed that enterprise is only one of the solutions for young people's integration. There are other options.
- Other places of integration could be opened up by placing more emphasis on individual plans targeted on self-employment.

- More emphasis could be placed on opportunities to develop projects in the context of the social economy, cooperatives or other forms of association.
- Young people's creativity needs to be stimulated by active methods, especially mentoring in enterprise.
- The public authorities should play an active role and encourage enterprises to become involved in the training and integration of young people.
- The world of work and employment is very changeable: we need to be able to change at the same pace and even more to anticipate change. Young people's information systems, monitoring systems and employment observatories are nowadays increasingly necessary.

Prerequisites for on-the-job training for disadvantaged young people

In the first instance, many questions raised the issue of whether young people were interested in finding a job or even if it was possible to offer them a job in the medium term.

If, however, it is accepted that social integration is greatly helped by occupational integration, the — naturally — 'educational' role of enterprises needs to be examined.

Saying that enterprise is a key player in training:

- affirms that placing young people in a working situation is an attempt not to propagate teaching methods that have patently failed;
- gives meaning to what young people learn. Young people are motivated by the meaning, scope and social recognition provided by the actual practice of a job;
- assumes that placing young people in a working situation makes it possible for them to learn by working in a real situation.

Training is provided from working situations, in working situations, and by placing people in working situations.

Schemes in enterprise are intended to make young people aware of their training needs and to help them to relate differently to work.

Enterprises and the training of disadvantaged young people

1. It is sometimes difficult to forge partnerships with enterprises, especially small enterprises; employers' federations are often useful intermediaries; there are always heavy demands on enterprises and they may not be available. The fact that a formal partnership contract is necessary means that links have to be created with employers' observatories.

   Enterprises are nevertheless aware that young people's skills are better and they are more prepared for employment when they have been trained in an enterprise. In some cases, they take the opportunity to rethink their organisation.

2. Identifying training situations prior to training itself is seen as very difficult, or even in conflict with the characteristics of the target group. One educational strategy would be to create situations in the local environment and to encourage young people to find themselves by taking part in the running of towns with all the other players (politicians, public service).

3. There is now a greater need to create links between training in enterprise and training at school.

4. Vocational guidance can make use of enterprises provided that young people's plans are well defined and can be integrated in a global approach. Care needs, however, to be taken: genuine vocational guidance may be artificial at this age, especially taking account of the features of this target group.

5. Finding new activities for young people (social economy) that give them a role in society and help them to participate in collective action is fundamental.

Group proposals:

- Need to continue exchanges of resources between project teams (professional recruitment contracts, analysis of working situations, etc.).
- Placing the training of trainers on a formal footing, in particular their ability to enter into dialogue with enterprises about working and training situations.

Training of tutors in enterprise and more specifically the conditions under which they can be available for young people.

Workshop 6

How do actions fit into the local environment
(integrated approach, multi-player partnerships)?

How do actions fit into the local environment?

A Youthreach perspective

Bridget Moylan
Youthreach Dublin (IRL)

General description

Youthreach is a national programme which targets unemployed unqualified early school leavers, from 15 to 18 years of age. Youthreach is an integral part of the national programme of second chance education and training. Under its general umbrella there are 64 Youthreach centres, 45 Community Training Workshops and 27 traveller training.

Centres are operating throughout the country. By virtue of national coordination and a range of common actions, it operates as a federal second-chance schooling network.

While Youthreach is a national programme, centres are locally managed, responding to and addressing the needs of the young people. It provides a client-focus approach, so that provision is driven by the needs of the target group.

It is, however, understood that Youthreach is not the only solution to early school leaving, but is one of a chain of multi-players in a local and regional continuum of provision.

Young people in a given area are not the preserve of any single agency. It is our belief that providers should endeavour to establish cooperative arrangements in order to maximise the effectiveness of resources.

Youthreach centres are located nationally, in areas of high disadvantage and exclusion (urban and rural).

Objectives

- Personal and social development, increased self-esteem.
- Second-chance education and introductory level training.
- Promoting independence, personal autonomy and a pattern of lifelong learning.
- Integration into further education and training opportunities and the labour market.
- Social inclusion.

Funding

European Social Fund and the Exchequer.

Certification

National certification. NCVA [8] Foundation level, level 1 and up to level 2.

Junior certification — Department of Education and Science State examinations.

(Eastern Health Board Certification, Sports Certification).

---

[8] The National Council for Vocational Awards.

Methods

Learner-centres, trans-disciplinary education and training, with a strong emphasis on the development of the individual.

Ballyfermot — south-west Dublin
Brief demographic summary

- High unemployment, low income.
- Long-term unemployment.
- High number of lone-parent-headed households. (In 1991 one fifth of households — which was nearly double the national average.)
- Low educational achievement. (In 1991 65.6 % of the population left school by the age of 15 or under. less than 1 % stayed in education until the age of 20 or over.)
- 1 % of the total population has attended 3rd level education through the history of Ballyfermot.
- Poor provision of amenities/facilities.
- Ballyfermot has an economic dependency rate (DE) of 3.1 compared to the national figure of 2.1 and the regional figure of 1.9.
- The Combat Poverty Agency ranks all of Ballyfermot as 10 on a scale of 1 to 10 for disadvantage.
- Badly affected by drug misuse and crime.

Example of integrated approach

Project — Production of CD Album of songs.

Youthreach Ballyfermot

The following organisations and bodies participated in various ways to ensure the success of our music project.

Youthreach Ballyfermot — VEC

1. *Department of Education & Science* (ESF section): Additional funding, encouragement and support.
2. *Local and national radio stations:* Interviews, airplay, and advertising.
3. *Local and national press:* Interviews, advertising coverage.
4. *Dublin cooperation:* Additional funding, use of local centre for performances, performances in local community events.
5. *School (3rd level) Senior College:* Guidance and advice for experts in rock college, use of studio, video team to record band's performances and launch.
6. *Psychological services:* Counselling for personal trauma for band members.
7. *Local and city private enterprise:* Additional funding.
8. *Police/JLO:* Funding, contributions, help with fundraising events.
9. *W.H.A.D.:* Use of mini-bus.
10. *Ballyfermot Partnership:* Performances at partnership events.
11. *Local employment services:* Invitation to perform at their launch (September).
12. *Eastern health board:* Support.
13. *Employers:* Funding contributions.
14. *Church:* Advertising.
15. *Youthreach Centres, Dublin:* Use of photographic and video resources. Help in fundraising events. Performances/Workshops.
16. *Youthreach (outside Dublin):* Workshops, performances in centres.
17. *Youthreach services:* Support, planned workshops/peer education in June 1998.
18. *Teachers Club of Ireland:* Use of premises for fundraising events.

Elefsina: An integrated local approach for the social and occupational integration of young people

Pinelopi Stathakopoulou
IEKEP

The problem of the occupational and social integration of young people at local level is very complex. In order to deal with it in the Elefsina approach we had to take into account at least three dimensions:

(a) the situation of young people;
(b) the labour market conditions;
(c) the commitment and resources at local area level to deal with the problem.

Insofar as the first dimension is concerned, certain factors increase the risk of social exclusion. These include:

1. Children from low socioeconomic status, single-parent families.
2. Children who face social, cultural and language barriers due to a migrant family background or minority status.
3. Girls and young women who are more numerous among unemployed youth populations.
4. Truancy and early school leaving before completing the compulsory level of education. This is related to lack of motivation, poor academic performance, and family breakdown as much as a lack of proper services and institutional support. Such children have very few chances of becoming socially integrated. They are faced with long-term unemployment, social alienation and delinquency.

With regard to the labour market:

1. Although in the industrialised urban areas, there are practically no jobs for unskilled or semi-skilled workers, the labour market in Greece can absorb untrained workers in low skill menial jobs.
2. An important factor, in relation to employment, is the dynamic of the local labour market, the quality and extent of the social networks which influence the chances of access to employment of young people with low levels of schooling.
3. Small-sized, family businesses provide more opportunities for employing unskilled, inexperienced young people than the large enterprises which place emphasis on trained workers, bureaucratic structures and a maximisation of profits.

Finally, as far as the third dimension is concerned:

1. The problem of the socioeconomic integration of youth requires a sustained, long-term effort and resources which are not always available at local community level. Funds from the central government or the European Union, in addition to meeting actual costs for local programmes, provide a strong incentive for the collaboration and participation of local agencies in such programmes.
2. Unemployment, as well as the awareness that the formulation of broad policies regarding social exclusion should be made at European Union level. The local areas have a very significant role to play to the extent that they have immediate access to the data, the causes and consequences of youth unemployment and social disintegration. It is at the local community level that the effectiveness of policies designed at the top are tested.

3. The local authority departments must be willing and able to participate in inter-agency coordination, structures and activities in order to respond to the needs of projects concerning the social and occupational integration of young people.
4. There must be a better understanding among community agencies and local officials about the seriousness of the problem of unemployment and social exclusion of young people, as well as the need to take necessary action at the local level to improve the situation.
5. The Community Development approach which was adopted at Elefsina, has shown that the identification of appropriate social partners, their mobilisation and commitment to take action requires considerable effort, professional involvement and knowledge of community development methods as well as ample time for the process to work.
6. The Elefsina project indicates the importance and makes explicit reference regarding the use of community organisation methodology to deal with the problems of social and occupational integration of young people.

   This implies:

   • coordination of local services and the development of appropriate structures for planning and service delivery;
   • participation and mobilisation of citizens and empowerment of target groups for problem solving;
   • use of trained staff in community organisation.
7. Important conditions for the success of local projects include legitimacy being granted by local agencies in order to initiate a project, as well as their involvement and their active support during all phases of the project.

The Elefsina project, has built on EU-backed projects. The benefits of such an approach are many. Local agencies get to know each other, build mutual trust and increase their programme planning and implementation skills. With every new project they are more easily convinced of the need to collaborate, to commit resources and to seek mutually satisfying outcomes.

Villa Fridhem
Härnösand, Sweden

Orving Gunnar
Aurora borealis

Cultural background — Härnösand

Härnösand is one of the oldest cities in central and northern Sweden (the municipality has 27 000 inhabitants). For 200 years it has been a centre for education and trade in the region. Nowadays, the faster growing industrial cities in the vicinity have taken over in many sectors, but Härnösand still retains its place in the field of education (Mid-Sweden University, a National Centre for Adult Distance Learning, National School for the Deaf, Residential College for Musical Studies, etc.). The County Administrative Board is situated in Härnösand and it is equally the Diocese of the region.

Structural changes in the economy

Due to economic reasons, structural changes have taken place within both the regions and municipalities in Sweden. The unemployment rates are higher in remote and peripheral areas than in the southern part of Sweden. Like other parts of Europe this has resulted in large numbers of unemployed: young people, women and disadvantaged individuals who do not have useful qualifications. Such people are dependent on social benefits of various kinds, they may be in training courses and schemes, but have uncertain future prospects. Local authorities, central government and voluntary organisations have made considerable efforts to alleviate the situation and bring down the present unemployment rate among disadvantaged groups.

The history of Villa Fridhem

Villa Fridhem vas built in 1868 by E. Wilhelm Kempe (shipowner and business magnate) as a gift for his wife Henriette. It was a summer dwelling for the family and the estate contained several buildings, an annex, quarters for maids and farmhands, storage, a dance pavilion and bathing facilities. Every summer the family packed up their belongings and furniture and moved for a three months stay in their summer residence. (In those days it was common among the upper-classes to have large summer houses and to visit each other for leisure and games.)

Since the 19th century the Kempe family has had a great impact on the timber industry along the coast of Norrland. They owned vast forests, invested in the saw-mill industry and started shipping wood products abroad. The saw-mill era was, in the middle of the 20th century, first supplemented and then taken over by the wood pulp industry and trade. Now the pulp processes have become more and more mechanised and automated and far fewer workers are needed. This forms part of the general picture of unemployment in Europe today. And so the Villa Fridhem project is a new link in the chain that binds together the different periods of development in the Härnösand region.

The Villa Fridhem project

During the autumn of 1993 the municipality of Härnösand, the owner of Villa Fridhem, had to make a choice. The buildings were in very bad condition and there was no use for them. However they were beautiful and precious buildings encapsulating a great deal of local culture and history. The usual means of restoration would have required a great deal of capital investment. The alternative was to pull the buildings down.

The present project leader was informed of the plans and began an initiative to save the buildings. He succeeded getting funds allocated for an alternative form of restoration. The Villa Fridhem project was established by a decision of the local authorities in January 1994. This decision was based on the fact that there was a need for a work place for people who for various reasons were at risk of being excluded from the labour market. The property was placed at the disposal of Social Services for a period or five years during which time the houses were to be restored and disadvantaged people at the same time would receive training and work. Since it was a classified building, regional antiquarians showed interest in the project and promised to support the action. The project leader had a clear vision of restoring the residence by employing the same working methods as were originally used.

This vision has been transformed into work plans for the buildings and the parks, as well as for individual training methods for the people involved. Actions have been approached in a step-by-step manner (projects) and financed accordingly.

However, the restoration of the classified buildings is only one of many projects that fall under the 'Villa Fridhem' heading. Others include, the recycling of material from waste, forestry, sawmill work, building and construction, carpentry, a blacksmiths forge, parks and gardens horticulture, information services, etc. The starting date and the pace of these projects depends on the interests and qualifications of the workers involved. The restoration has proceeded since autumn 1994 and has engaged both local craftsmen and regional restoration experts. Funding has been forthcoming from local authorities (personnel costs of trainers and staff), from regional authorities (preservation expertise) and EU funding (Objectives 3 and 4). Close cooperation has been maintained with the Social Services sector in the community and with the local employment agency.

'Creating value renders value'

All involved are actively engaged in individual training that is based around the concept of 'normality', i.e., participation is mixed, irrespective of age, sex, previous knowledge, etc., and with the notion that everyone has the ability to cope with what has to be done and that everyone is expected to take full responsibility for their work.

The motto for work at Villa Fridhem is 'Creating value renders value'.

According to the usual interpretation of 'work' it is a means used by man to obtain tangible assets. Within the Villa Fridhem project a more meaningful interpretation is preferred in which 'work' has three functions:

1. it provides opportunities for being with others (very important)
2. it provides opportunities for doing something valuable in the community
3. it provides an opportunity to earn a living.

1. *'Samverkansprojektet'*

Last year the Swedish National Board for Youth Affairs was commissioned by the Government to conduct, a cooperation development project known as *Samverkansprojektet,* in selected pilot municipalities. These projects have the aim of strengthening preventive actions aimed at disadvantaged youth. The Municipality of Härnösand applied for participation and was accepted as one of the five projects in Sweden. This three-year project will start in August 1998.

All political parties in Härnösand have joined in the integrated action to improve the future of the community/municipality. Different strategies and methods, crucial to development in Härnösand have been agreed on. Methods and models for successfully combating exclusion in disadvantaged groups is one of the strategic and long term areas of development.

The scope of the *Samverkansprojektet* in Härnösand

The intentions of the municipality are to formulate a programme of cooperation between local authorities and organisations with the aim of developing a model for early detection and support; to develop an action-centred integration of resources in the educational sector and the social services; to develop specific programmes for integration into upper secondary school level, adult education and '*Kunskapslyftet*' in order to provide young people (up to the age of 25) with the opportunity of combining additional theoretical training with hands-on vocational training at a local work centre (Villa Fridhem); to develop close cooperation between the project and local employment efforts being made in the municipality.

Partners:

The project is run by the Municipality of Härnösand.

The main partners are the Villa Fridhem Cooperative, local school authorities and local social services authorities.

Other partners include: the Härnösand Youth Council, the Härnösand Adult Education Institutes, local social partners, trade unions, the local trade and industry organisations, the regional Committee for the Building Trade and Construction, the regional architect, the regional restoration specialist, local police authorities and the local Employment Agency.

The innovative feature of this project is that cooperation with the educational sector is in the forefront. It is based on an integrated approach (at individual level) and on cross-sector cooperation (at organisational level). It is in line with strategies for further raising local awareness and experience and for further developing the attributes of the Villa Fridhem work centre. The project will serve as a basis for new local development projects as well as for the on-going adaptation of training programmes and training plans. It will equally serve as a basis for a new economic structure for cooperation between different sectors of the local community.

The programme focuses on individual and group development from secondary school level up to the age of 25. Individuals will participate in long-term training programmes including integrated and on-going counselling. The aim of the programme is to offer individuals the opportunity to live a normal life, to be able to take responsibility for themselves and to play an active part in development within the community. Upper secondary school skills with full certification for all those involved is the fundamental objective.

The *Samverkansprojektet* programme

The integration of resources by the aforementioned partners makes it possible to enter into contact with young people at an early stage (early detection). The development of 'personal projects' has the aim of channelling young people's creativity and energy in a desirable direction. Integration makes it possible to provide such individuals with an understanding of their cultural heritage and a basis for their personal development. Group dynamics will further strengthen the ability of individuals to control their situation and the meaningfulness of the work carried out will increase the self-esteem and confidence of participants. The model for this action stems from the ideas of Professor A. Antonovsky, concerning the health factors that support personal development.

The central concept of the model is a sense of coherency, of comprehensibility, manageability and meaningfulness.

Antonovsky defines the model as follows: 'The sense of coherency is a global attitude that expresses to what extent the individual has a thorough, permanent and dynamic sense of confidence that the stimuli originating from the internal and external world throughout different stages of his life are structured, foreseeable and understandable (comprehensibility), that the resources needed to match the demands these stimuli place on the individual are actually available, that the demands are considered as challenging and worth the investment and commitment.'

The cooperation project has various sub-programmes for different target and age groups: secondary school, upper secondary school and young adults who have left education without finishing studies. The practical training, integrated into upper secondary and adult education, will be carried out at the Villa Fridhem work centre. It will be closely linked to specific parts of the ECO environment programme curriculum, the Cultural Heritage programme and the Adventure/Sensation programme, all of these are linked to varying degrees with tourism and entrepreneurship.

As has been mentioned, the basic idea behind Villa Fridhem is one of 'normality' and the new *'Samverkansprojektet'* project will develop the step-by-step means for integrating groups of young people threatened by exclusion into groups of local partners in different areas who are cooperating to produce the future welfare of Härnösand.

Integrated training schemes

Laurent Wattelet
Ministry of Education
Integration Unit, Lille (F)

Description of integrated training

Integrated training is a scheme run by the *Mission Générale d'Insertion* (General Integration Unit) of the French Ministry of Education and I should like, by way of introduction, to describe the work of the *Mission Générale d'Insertion*.

The Mission Générale d'Insertion covers all secondary schools in France. The Mission makes it possible to take rapid action:

- that uses lightweight structures that are accommodated in schools,
- that is very flexible since schemes are fully in keeping with the host facility and its economic environment,
- that has a limited life, as schemes last from nine weeks to three years,
- that involves high levels of alternatives, as at least 50 % of each scheme involves training in enterprise,
- that is for a target group which is failing or has dropped out of school after compulsory education (age 16).

All these principles form part of integrated training. Schemes are negotiated with schools, generally vocational *lycées*. They are alternative schemes in specific sectors of activity and are aimed at those young people facing the worst qualification problems; they last three years and have two main stages.

During the first stage, generally lasting one year, young people have school status. The aim is to consolidate the young person's career plan and to obtain a qualification contract. This is a period of trial and observation for both the enterprise and the young person.

The second stage, lasting two years, involves a contract of employment enabling the young person to acquire a qualification recognised by a certificate, in this case the *Certificat d'Aptitudes Professionnelles* (Certificate of Vocational Aptitude). During both stages, training is supervised by a coordinator.

The integrated training, of which I am coordinator, is taking place in the clothing production sector in the north of France in the small town of Caudry close to Cambrai. Fifteen or so young people and the same number of enterprises are involved and we are currently in the first stage of training.

Review of the origins of the scheme, target group, content and the teaching methods used

Origins of the scheme:

This project was set up for three reasons:

1. The fact that an association of clothing production enterprises wishing to find better motivated and better qualified staff had detected a shortage of initial-level skilled staff.
2. Solutions needed to be found for the socio-occupational integration of a group of young people in a rural environment with problems of geographical mobility.
3. Cooperation between enterprises and the Ministry of Education needed to be stepped up to provide a solution in terms of training, qualification and integration.

The target group:

Young people aged over 16, with few social reference points, very far from obtaining an initial qualification and in particular lacking any job prospects, form the target group for this integrated training.

Content and teaching methods used

The integrated training run by the *Mission Générale d'Insertion* forms part of the French education system. Alternative methods are set up in a way that suits enterprises and is in keeping with the availability of the teachers who have volunteered for this scheme. At the Jacquard vocational school, for instance, young people attend classes on Mondays and Tuesdays and spend Wednesdays, Thursdays and Fridays in an enterprise.

The following subjects are taught: French, mathematics, knowledge of the contemporary world, communications, knowledge of enterprise and vocational education. During this first stage of integrated training there is no reference standard, making it possible for us to work towards specific objectives which include:

- remedial work on basic skills in mathematics and French,
- developing civic responsibility through the 'contemporary world',
- acquiring skills in communications and knowledge of enterprise operation so that trainees can make the most of their periods in enterprise and work, for instance, on social skills,
- acquiring basic skills in clothing production through vocational education; the responsibilities of the Ministry of Education and enterprises for the training of these young people are set out in a specification drawn up by both parties at the beginning of the first stage,
- developing personal training for each young person that depends on his or her training enterprise,
- work on all issues concerning the professional world and enterprises.

The whole of the teaching team also avoids anything that smacks of the 'conventional education system'. Allowing everyone to work at their own pace and fostering students' personal development are the main aims; everyone's expectations can then be met in the best possible way. The fact that we have used a small voluntary teaching team, who will supervise the young people right up to completion of the second stage, has made this result possible.

The general principle of the teaching that students receive in this integrated training is that it breaks away from methods that were previously unsuited to these young people without, however, abandoning our objectives of occupational integration and qualification.

The partnership

The main partner in this integrated training is obviously enterprise. If the scheme is to be successful, enterprises have to commit themselves to:

- providing the young people with an opportunity to find out about jobs by carrying them out,
- offering jobs that are on a par with the jobs of other employees so that students can implicitly be considered as full members of the enterprise,
- playing their part in ensuring that the school and the enterprise are working towards the same goals by passing on information to teachers, via the coordinator, about their professional expectations,
- helping to design the content of the training by drawing up a specification for each enterprise,
- in particular providing young people with a bridge to the second stage, i.e. with opportunities for integration into the enterprise.

The other partners are chiefly the information and guidance centre and the information and guidance offices which help to find the young people when the project is being set up. The GRETA, which is a group of schools at which continuing training qualifications can be obtained and where training can be continued without changing teachers, also plays a part and provides these young people with a much more reassuring view of the future.

Monitoring in enterprise

Monitoring the young people in enterprise is an integral part of the work of the integrated training coordinator since he is the main person with whom the enterprise tutors deal. He also allocates the young people to the various enterprises taking account of geographical constraints (most of the young people are dependent on transport company infrastructure) as well as the profile that has been worked out with the enterprise and the future tasks that the young person will have to carry out. He is also responsible for tying up any loose ends when the agreement between the young person and the enterprise has come to an end.

The coordinator therefore visits the enterprises and the young people's workplaces in order to assess their progress and to deal with any problems that may have arisen.

Monitoring takes place together with the young person's tutor, using datasheets based on each enterprise's specification in order to ensure that the training plan is being fully implemented. Any changes in the enterprise tutor's expectations can also be recorded in these datasheets which can then be passed on to the teaching team so that future work by the school and the enterprise is as consistent as possible.

Monitoring generally involves one visit per month. The coordinator can always be contacted by the enterprises, for instance to report an absence, deal with inappropriate behaviour, implement any additional training that may be necessary and therefore amend the initial plan as the year progresses.

The coordinator also has to keep in close touch with the enterprises in order to set up training projects; in the scheme for which I am responsible, for instance, the young people wanted to make a video film about their training experiences; the enterprises did not just accept this plan but themselves proposed to extend the plan by making another film about the professional methods that they were using.

This monitoring is extremely important as it means that successful training can be built on by reviewing, together with the young person, what progress has been made, what efforts have been put into it and by making the young person aware that he or she is able to carry out tasks that seemed impossible at the beginning of the training.

The resources mobilised

The resources mobilised are chiefly human, organisational and financial.

Human resources include:

1. The creation of a part-time coordinator's job at the host school; working with the school principal, the coordinator sets up and monitors all the training. The coordinator's tasks are to:
    * keep the young people motivated,
    * support their plans,
    * ensure that the school and enterprises are working towards the same goals,
    * lead and coordinate the teaching team,
    * meet families and keep them informed about their child's progress.

2. The allocation of one tutor per enterprise who, on the basis of his or her occupational experience, can build up the young person's vocational skills by:
    * choosing working situations that offer scope for advancement and training in accordance with the training plan,
    * passing on know-how and an enterprise culture,
    * taking part in the monitoring of the young person and reviewing changes in behaviour,
    * establishing a relationship of trust with the young person that generates greater motivation.

3. The teaching team, made up of volunteer teachers from the school interested in an innovative strategy, who help, throughout the training, to build on expertise and knowledge from an educational point of view and in particular to formulate a personal and differentiated route with the coordinator and the tutors.

The organisational resources that the scheme draws on are the facilities of the host vocational *lycée;* if an integrated training scheme is to be successful, the school principal has to want to help young people who are not at ease in traditional education to achieve a qualification.

Other resources are implicitly all the other resources available in a vocational *lycée*: vocational education workshops, computers and specific software for clothing production, cameras, video laboratory, etc.

From the point of view of financial resources, the total cost of an integrated training scheme is of FRF 176 100, i.e. approximately ECU 26 650, which breaks down as follows:

*   human resources: FRF 166 350, i.e. ECU 25 100
    (part-time coordinator's job, teachers' pay)
*   operating costs: FRF 9750, i.e. ECU 1470,
    (administrative costs).

The innovative nature of the scheme

In the integrated training scheme in clothing production at the Jacquard vocational *lycée* in Caudry, the approach taken is one of providing personalised training in keeping with the young person's learning abilities and the expectations of his or her enterprise and more generally of placing the emphasis on the individual. Setting up this kind of educational and behavioural scheme was important because Caudry is located in a rural environment where failure at school for young people without qualifications often leads to inactivity and reliance on the welfare State.

Its first innovative character is that it breaks away from the conventional approach: training and then integration which has done little to help these students, and replaces it with integration and then training, making it possible to help these young people to regain their confidence and to make them more aware of the benefits of the training on offer, i.e. to make them into training seekers.

In addition:

*   it is a negotiated scheme,
*   it includes 'made to measure' training,
*   training is run with the support of families.

Workshop 6

How do actions fit into the local environment (integrated approach, multi-player partnerships)?

Summary of the two sessions on this topic

Rudolf Mondelaers, Berufsfortbildungswerk (BFW), Berlin (D)
Vítor Soares, Regional Development Agency of Setubal (P)

Introduction

Three projects concerning the integration of socially disadvantaged young people into the local environment were presented at Workshop 6:

1. The Dublin Youthreach project (Ireland).
2. The IEKEP project of the town of Elefsina (Greece).
3. The Swedish 'Villa Fridhem' project.

Solutions and conditions for the successful integration of target groups

Solutions for the integration of target groups into the mainstream development of our society are more effective and efficient when they are based on consensus and treated as integral parts of local development. This means:

*   In the first instance, that they have educational and vocational training profiles and objectives that take strict account of the needs of the local area. This may include, for instance, training young people to set up horse-riding schools as in the case of young prisoners in Ireland, or even integrating the training scheme into a 'ecological' context as in Sweden. In this context, local training profiles at a relatively low level of qualification may play a positive role.
*   Second, that these profiles and objectives allow for sustainable local development. As the motto of the 'Villa Fridhem' project puts it: 'creating value renders value'.

The success of such projects depends to a large extent on the possibility of creating stable local partnerships or networks with all local players and institutions. These networks make it possible to bring together and mobilise all local resources and potential for young people's integration. Several conditions need to be satisfied if these partnerships are to work in practice. For instance:

(a) project personnel need to be trained to manage these networks. In the Greek project, for instance, trainers receive training in the following areas:
    *   statistical and socioeconomic analysis to identify blackspots and deficits as well as political, social, cultural, ethnic and economic resources that are available and can be mobilised at local level;
    *   drawing up local development plans and implementing local projects;
    *   leading and promoting local networks;
    *   evaluation using locally defined evaluation criteria.
(b) involving the local population in projects through information campaigns, consensual decision-making and formal and informal coordination methods that are as far-reaching as possible;
(c) interesting the authorities in projects and involving them from the outset;
(d) ensuring that young people play an active part in decision-making;
(e) showing the young people involved in the experiment that they can bring about change locally.

The aim, therefore, is to develop methods and teaching practices that take account of local structures and are therefore locally adapted.

There is a strong correlation between the difficulties that an area is facing and the problems of its young people. Institutions consequently have little capacity for the creation of local networks or partnerships for young people's integration.

Cooperation between schools and enterprises through local network projects is nevertheless of key importance. In the case of the projects presented, a number of problems identified at this stage were discussed.

In the case of the Greek project, for instance, it was pointed out that the problem of re-integrating socially disadvantaged young people had been largely underestimated. In the town of Elefsina, for instance, a high proportion (40 % according to some experts) of young people were failing to complete compulsory education. Causes included the problems faced by schools in controlling this type of problem and in particular the difficulties of forging close links with the world of work.

Generally, cooperation between schools and authorities is problematic. It works better when projects contain modules that prepare young people for re-integration into normal school life. In the case of the Greek project, there was a re-integration rate of 70 %.

The school/enterprise partnership can also prove to be very difficult, especially if the local economy is in recession when more time is needed to set up the partnership and provide it with an organisational structure.

Proposals for network creation

The following topics and methods were proposed for networking:

(a) Creating integrated project networks on the long-term prevention of failure at school is a necessity.
(b) Creating networks that do not concentrate on the acquisition of general or vocational knowledge, but on individual, collective or social learning about work at local level would be useful. This would help to foster an attitude towards the development of the local community based on an integrated approach.
(c) An approach that tries to re-integrate adolescents into the education and training system needs to be combined with an analysis of the changes that need to be made to this system to make it more attractive.
(d) Improved coordination and cooperation with Ministries and other local authorities — and between agencies — needs to be sought.
(e) Establishing networks of and between different European structures, in particular DGs V, VI, XVI, XXII and XXIII of the European Commission, is desirable.
(f) Conducting a detailed study of the levels of power at which 'second chance' issues are tackled in the various European countries. In some countries, decisions are made at local or regional level and in others at national level. This study should help to clarify the possibilities for network cooperation.

Part IV

Action for young people's integration: Networking and transnational cooperation

Plenary Session
8 May

European coordination of the 'Second Chance School' pilot projects

Jean-François Mézières
(AFPA — DUE)

We all know in theory and even more so in practice that the European Union has millions of young people who are cut off from education and training systems and excluded from the labour market. It is in order to tackle this situation, which cannot be perceived as inevitable, that the guidelines of Objective 3 'combating exclusion' were included in the White Paper on teaching and learning: towards the learning society. Second Chance School projects come at the top of these guidelines.

It seems important to me to stress that forging close links between innovative initiatives and consolidated experiences will promote very valuable exchanges that pave the way for concrete cooperation between different partners who are all concerned to offer a new chance to those young people who need it and to help to them to make the 'new start' recommended by the conclusions of the Luxembourg summit on employment.

While many networks already exist and our meeting is not the first of its type, the aim is to forge links between initiatives having many common features.

I think it is possible now to pinpoint identical features from the information sheets describing all the projects represented at this conference.

One of the main features that they have in common is that they all focus on the target group of young people who have left the conventional education system without the essential learning that they need usefully to benefit from qualifying training schemes and to make sustainable progress in employment. Moreover, and despite their differences, four features frequently recur in the schemes launched under the generic name of 'second chance schools':

(a) a **solid partnership** between all the local partners and in particular enterprises that can recruit young people (the economic actors);
(b) **innovative teaching methods shaped by young people's needs**: the school does not have all the answers, but acts as a focus making it possible to provide a personal response for each young person as a whole that takes account of his or her strengths and weaknesses;
(c) a highly involved, qualified, motivated and experienced leadership team with multi-disciplinary skills. From vocational guidance to support for active job-finding strategies, these workers are active at every stage and provide training, education, counselling and aid and, in some cases, are tutors in enterprises;
(d) the **key role of the new educational technologies**: computers and multimedia play a key role in these projects. It is evident that these tools provide a new and motivating environment for these young people whose experience up to now has been marked by failure. In addition, this approach makes it possible to network with other sites and to profit from exchanges of experience.

Lastly, all the initiatives and experiences that we have discussed are taking place in disadvantaged areas and problematic districts especially in the suburbs of major urban areas; these projects have been developed at the focus of the world's problems where cultures are mixed together, families broken up and drugs are a major drama. While there may be many handicaps, each of the projects shows that there are genuine reasons for hope.

In order to consolidate the links that have been forged at this conference, I propose to structure our community around the Second Chance Schools Internet site that we intend to build together as a part of a project financed by DG XIII and run by the European Vocational Training Association.

In coming weeks, everyone will be able to consult this resource free of charge; the following services will be available:

(a) information sheets on and addresses of all the projects presented at this conference;
(b) an interactive electronic mail site (everyone can have a free mailbox on the network) making it possible to circulate information and take part in forums;
(c) regular publication of news of our network.

These two days represent the starting point of the second strand of the 'Second Chance Schools' pilot project; without wishing to anticipate the conclusions of our work, I feel that there are two main questions to be tackled:

1. Over and above summary sheets and workshops, how can we make our experiences more legible and visible?
2. How can we organise genuinely efficient exchanges and transfers?

Experience shows mutual understanding takes time. In this respect, the construction of a network is a major investment. A shared language is also necessary and I feel that we have started to pave the way for such a language since yesterday.

Tools are also needed to facilitate exchanges and communications; the Second Chance Schools Internet site should, I hope, provide these tools.

This will be no more than the embryo of a future telematic network. Much more can obviously be done in the future and will largely depend on yourselves and the added value that the network provides for each of your experiments. During the start-up phase of the network, each project officer taking part in the 'second strand' is entitled to an electronic address and can use the electronic mail service of our network. The resource is there, but it is up to you to bring it to life, make it useful and enhance it. Without this network, the second strand of the Second Chance Schools would be no more than a series of interesting, warm and stimulating conferences. With the network, I feel that we will be able to build an efficient network serving those young people in the European Union who are currently excluded from knowledge, employment and ultimately society.

By way of conclusion to this brief talk, I should like to say a few words about the experiment constituted by the 12 new educational sites known as the first strand of the Second Chance Schools project. After selection from a number of projects put forward by local authorities, we now have 12 schools, half of which have opened, and 12 projects that share the features that I described earlier but which do not in any way follow a standard model. I should like to give a few examples that help to illustrate the features of these pilot projects.

In Bilbao, training is spread over two years and divided into three stages in which increasing emphasis is placed on learning in enterprise. The school, which was inaugurated last November, has very high-powered multimedia equipment.

The Marseilles school has opened as well: the main feature of this project is that a contract is signed by the student, the school and the enterprise that will be the future employer: a job is therefore available and guaranteed from the outset. Training can then be focused on this job.

In Hämeenlinna in Finland, the school is more a place for reception and guidance, helping young people to make the best possible use of existing vocational training facilities.

This pilot project network has been being built up for a year. Overall, I should like to stress — although everyone here has had this experience — that communication and comprehension raise problems when pooling experiences and developing exchanges: these are not just problems of language but problems connected with the organisational and conceptual complexity of our area of work. It would be naïve to think that efficient communication is possible after a few hours of meetings and even more naïve to expect genuine transfers of good practice and teaching methods.

This makes up the first strand of the Second Chance Schools project. The impact of these various projects is undoubtedly symbolic in the first instance: while they make no claim to provide all the answers, they lie at the heart of the problems and show that solutions are possible.

We have been able to set in motion a dialogue and exchanges on each of the topics covered by the workshops. The telematic facilities that we are making available will help us to pursue and build on these; I can do no more than encourage you to ensure that everyone is able to profit from experiments under way in a network made up of a wide range of initiatives all of which share, however, the wish to help all young people whose first experience of education did not pave the way for their integration and did not enable them to find their place in society, to regain their confidence.

European cooperation in the European virtual training college

Christoph Harnischmacher
Ulrich Rauter

Introduction

The following presentation of the Socrates EVA project particularly focuses on the relationship between open learning and *Lernzielorientierter Unterricht* in the European collaborative process. It highlights the question of the compatibility of virtual classrooms and real classrooms when used with disadvantaged young people. We look back on the EVA project that started at the end of 1995 and attempt to evaluate the main difficulties and the more unexpected results.

Project partners from Germany (IMBSE E.V.), Spain (AID) and the Netherlands (PPI) are working together with the EVA project aimed at young people. It is attempting to develop a method of open and distance learning that reflects the special needs of this target group.

Being disadvantaged

What does it mean to be disadvantaged? Is it possible to identify the main characteristics of a disadvantaged individual? There are many of different factors today that combine in making a young person 'disadvantaged'.

Firstly, I would like to underline that being 'disadvantaged' is in direct relation to the social situation of the young people and that it is not the result of the personal characteristics of the individual as such. As we are now witnessing, increased youth unemployment is generating ever greater social selection phenomena. While young people were in a position to make clear-cut decisions with regard to their working lives even 10 years ago, today they cannot have much expectation for continued employment. Take an immigrant youth from Turkey living in Moers, for example, and coming from a family who left their native country in the 1960s because the husband found employment in one of the mines in Moers. Today, the traditional mining environment does not hold out any such hopes for the future, the mines have been closed down and the miners made redundant or sent into early retirement. Such Turkish youths neither possess their own indigenous Turkish culture nor are they fully integrated and accepted members of the German regional community — be it language-wise or culturally. When placed in competition with German youths they usually stand a poor chance, since the demand for training places is much higher than the number of training opportunities on offer.

Existing social conditions and individual situations powerfully interact with each other, spiralling the marginalisation of certain social groups. In relation to the Socrates EVA project, our national situation reflects what we individually and nationally determine as being the 'disadvantaged' target groups at local level. In this respect, the term 'disadvantaged' is relative. We now tend to abstain from (and request others to do the same) from terming people as 'disadvantaged' because of the danger of stigmatising the individuals concerned, i.e. by projecting social consequences as actually being the qualities of that individual *sui generis*.

Social design

This is the complex and multi-layered social context in which the EVA project is set. In contrast to the classical ODL situation which appeals more to university-type learners, we find that the learner's personality, his or her social heritage and integration is crucial to their personal definition of meaningful educational targets and achievements. The classical form of distance learning is based on an ideal learner who is intrinsically motivated and will study on their own account and independently. Under such circumstances distance learning offers the advantage of overcoming spatial distance so that subjects can be taught, i.e., a curriculum can be provided which would not otherwise be available locally. The official translation of 'distance learning' in German is *'Fernunterricht'* which particularly highlights the paradigm of this type of distance learning as a *distribution of knowledge*. Looking at the target groups that we have in our projects, however, the underlying social premises of classical distance learning come into clearer focus and with it the incompatibility of this somewhat academic mode of teaching when compared to the requirements, interests and skills of our target groups.

Within the scope of the EVA project, ODL more than anything else means offering a different set of subjects as well as providing an alternative to standard classroom learning which has already disappointed a great many of these young people.

The EVA project is rooted in the real world classroom, so that it is possible to transfer the social context to the virtual classroom. This is a fundamental thesis of the EVA project and reflects the fact that young people depend on receiving personal and social assistance as well as getting motivating support and encouragement.

Another fundamental thesis of the EVA project is the conviction that it is not so much a lack of technical development which stands in the way of using modern means of communication, but that it is pedagogical integration that must be given priority. This is why we gave preference to commercially available tools such as multimedia software for stand-alone PCs and Internet tools which favour the transfer of the project's results.

In practice the development and maintenance of the Internet environment for the virtual classroom involved a great deal of work. The development of the project covered the following phases:

Project phases — From open to distance learning

Phase 1: Transfer of software design by learners

During the first year, all partners familiarised themselves with the multimedia tools in local multimedia studios. Jointly with the young people, the partners developed products by following the *Software Design by Learners* method *(SDL)*. We provide learners with the software tools. The young people then create audiovisual, biographical and content-centred collages in the multimedia studios using a local network and multimedia tools. By expressing themselves creatively they become actors on the European stage. In this process they make use of communication tools, production and design tools and other software resources.

The outcome was various applications and pedagogical concepts, based on the different regional structures and contexts. It had been our basic idea to place young people in the position of being able to express situations that were of importance to them, via multimedia presentations, thus encouraging them to get involved in a deeper learning processes. In this respect, our project resulted in a target-group oriented form of open learning.

Phase 2: from OL to ODL

In phase 2 we were concerned with Europe-wide networking of our local multimedia environments via the Internet. We divested the distance learning model of its university-like paradigm of knowledge distribution which only benefits *homo educandus*. In this way we translated the term 'distance learning' by the term 'cross-border learning' in order to stress the active and cooperation-oriented nature of EVA.

With cross-border open learning, open learning should not only occur in a local social context, it should then be transferred beyond the local situation through an active and cooperative European process: through the group work of young European learners and their educators. We particularly wanted to transcend cultural borders and linguistic barriers as we progressed towards a Europe of our own design.

To begin with, this of course meant the establishment of a suitable Internet environment as well as the creation of the necessary cooperation among the teachers involved. Before opening the virtual classroom, the virtual teachers' room had to be created. The following demonstrates the structure of the virtual classroom on the Internet.

The Internet environment

The processes are mediated by an EVA learning environment on the Internet. This supports the development of a community of learners in the virtual classroom. It needs to be a dynamic learning environment: a space for international communication and contact, for communicative and interactive international learning projects. Thanks to the Internet, text, images, data and sound can be exchanged and handled via the EVA *Eurokaleidoscopes* and *Personal Info Pages*.

The EVTC consists of different rooms modelled on a real school. In the virtual 'entrance hall' of the school an exhibition can be viewed before entering the actual work and communication areas. The first area, known as EXHIBITION in the menu controlled user interface of the system, contains general information on the EVTC project, on institutions and the people participating, as well as about the conceptual background and the motivation driving the project. This area is presented in the national language of each participating country. In all other areas of the EVTC only English is used.

In the on-line classroom, actual project work takes place and it forms the main work area for EVTC project participants.

In the on-line CLASSROOM the user finds various tools (NEWSLETTER and Personal Info pages (PIP)). The advantage of the NEWSLETTER as well as the PIPs is that even participants with little or no previous knowledge can intuitively publish on-line information about themselves or about interesting general or project-related topics, based on basic forms. In addition, with the help of forms, any multimedia document can be stored on the central EVTC server and accessed later. Other resources can be downloaded from the Internet for reference.

Other communication options are found in AULA and these go hand-in-hand with the work going on in the virtual CLASSROOM. A notice board is available for participants and teachers, and times and places for direct online exchanges (CHAT) can be agreed upon. In addition, the system provides each participant and work group with an e-mail address to enable them to send and receive. In AULA a list informs users of such addresses already assigned. Finally, an interactive list of interesting topics and project areas which are, or might be of interest, can be found under different headings.

The EVTC set-up is completed by an organisational area whose functions are combined in the TEACHERS' ROOM. For the time being, an interactive collection of discussion topics concerning the EVTC is planned (public news, similar to newsgroups on the Internet) as well as an up-to-date overview of the schedules in the EVTC.

Review of the project

We will go into more detail of the Internet environment since results in other areas are more interesting.

Four learning groups from the Netherlands, one from Spain and three from Germany participated in the EVTC project, with trainers and students collaborating on joint projects — Eurokaleidoscopes. These activities formed part of the regular training. Groups spent between four to eight hours weekly on the projects. What did students learn during the project? and What kind of skills did they develop? The Dutch evaluator summed it up thus: '... teachers mentioned a growing independence of students. The educational interactions changed from a student-teacher to student-student interactions and from teacher-centred to learner-centred education. The trainers became coaches. Apart from that there was a clear difference between the various PPI groups' [9].

Furthermore, the young people involved in the project developed better interpersonal and cooperative skills, much more so than in a traditional classroom setting. The teachers were also astonished by the technical competence shown by young people in the project. But teachers found it hard work adapting and initiating new approaches. This seems to be an important point in innovative work. The teachers also needed guidance in coping with the permanently changing paths of the open learning model.

But looking back we also need to emphasise the difficulties surrounding the European Virtual Classroom project. An honest stocktaking leads us to see the problematic side of the assumption on which the EVA project was based. The real classroom model is not just a means and a stepping-stone towards the virtual classroom, but because of its social structures and implied context it also generates limitations in relation to the full use of all the opportunities of Internet-based open learning. Time related dynamics of explorative and formative interaction are not compatible with the traditional principle of a timetable. The same holds true for teaching style as well as for the expectations and involvement in the learning process of young people. When transferring our experiment into on-line collaboration it is important for project managers and teachers to think about the parameters that make transnational group work successful. Such parameters must be woven into the design of a networked learning environment. Some of these parameters we will mention at the end of our presentation.

Transnational learning

- **Increasing workload**
  The day-to-day work of the respective institutions still has top priority for the teachers engaged in the project. The 'European work' is additional work, this means it is not only an enrichment but also an extra burden for teachers.

- **Jumping the language barriers**
  Communication in a foreign language was a major challenge for all actors in the project. Disadvantaged target groups particularly need intensive personal support in order to be able to participate in an environment of transnational intercommunication. Because of this we developed the 'English on-line' lessons which are to be tested in the 'Europlus' project of the Youthstart programme.

- **Differences in target groups**
  The national target groups across Europe are often not homogenous. 'At risk' is a very different concept in Ciudad Real than it is in Amsterdam. So one target group is likely to drop out while another may embark on quite a good career. In Amsterdam or Moers (Germany) students risk dropping out too, but their poor school record was more based on bad behaviour, social and learning problems. To coordinate pedagogical processes under varying circumstances is difficult.

- **Personal contacts**
  Meetings between young people are meaningful. Any transnational cooperation, which is based solely on on-line communication encounters problems of motivating students and involving them.

- **Time management**
  Continued cooperation between students over long periods of time is difficult to organise. Timetables, training phases and daily schedules are often not compatible with the different transnational contexts. During the project, six to eight week 'pilot phases' stood the test. During these phases local target groups were able to agree on a joint transnational schedules.

- **Continuous teacher communication**
  Without a continuous exchange of teacher's experience in the local context the transnational collabo-

---

[9] Burgos, Steffi: An evaluation of the participation of PPI, In The second year of EVTC, Amsterdam 1997, p. 4.

ration will fail. There must be on-line discussion between teachers in transnational projects in order to prepare target groups and provide adequate planning of cross-border activities.

- **ODL in closed structures**
  Equally, national educational systems differ. In some cases there are rigid training structures and in others open educational philosophies that allow for a great deal of trial and error. To implement an open learning system in a rigid educational structure you may have to struggle against resistance, and collaboration between project partners from different types of systems (open/closed) may prove difficult.

- **Institutional support**
  Management of training institutes has to adequately sustain the start-up of networked learning and the follow-up activities. If the management is not highly motivated in wishing to implement networked learning in day-to-day training, there may be many conflicts which will hinder such activities. The management together with the staff has to cooperate in developing both an open and creative atmosphere.

Annexes

Conference programme

Integrating young people into society through education and training, 7 and 8 May 1998

Hotel Bedford — Brussels

Background

Between 10 and 20 % of young people in the European Union (EU) leave the education system without any qualifications at all and 45.5 % of the 15–24 age group have only a low qualification, the equivalent of lower secondary level at most. Their possibilities to actively participate in society and their chances of getting into the labour market are very slim without basic qualifications or skills.

The White Paper 'Teaching and learning: towards the learning society', adopted by the Commission at the instigation of Mrs Edith Cresson and Mr Pádraig Flynn, stressed the need to focus special attention on the population groups in greatest difficulty, particularly young people, when contemplating a Union of knowledge.

Each of the Member States has, in the light of its own specific features, taken various steps to head off exclusion, sometimes with the support of Community programmes or initiatives. All in all, much has been done and successes have been notched up which have been sometimes remarkable and all too often underpublicised. A wider range of training channels has opened up, teaching approaches have diversified bringing the pupil back to the centre of the education process, schools and the business sector have drawn closer together and cooperated better, and programmes targeting young people aged 16–25 have been implemented.

The Directorate-General for Education, Training and Youth has followed up the guidelines put forward in the paper (Objective 3 'Combat exclusion') and in order to step up the fight against exclusion has undertaken a twofold initiative. Firstly, the Commission, in conjunction with the governments concerned, is providing support for a range of pilot projects to do with 'second chance schools'. Secondly, the Structural Funds (particularly the European Social Fund) and the Socrates (education) and Leonardo da Vinci (training) programmes have provided the framework for innovatory social and occupational integration projects. There is also the new European voluntary service for young people which is providing opportunities to young people for an original formative experience in other European countries whilst contributing to local development.

In parallel with the implementation of these pilot projects, it is necessary to build on the multitude of actions undertaken locally, nationally or at Community level and to network them in order to allow the results to produce a cascade effect, to identify the most relevant elements of transferability and to encourage fresh experiments.

An approach of this kind will put young unemployed persons at the heart of the debate, without forgetting that prevention is an essential and complementary strategy to reintegration. The start of this conference will therefore be given over to the analysis of dropping out and failure at school, and to identify good practices as prevention or remedy for the problem of failure at school among young people.

Objectives

This conference has a threefold objective:

• to examine the features and reasons for school failure;

- to assemble significant examples of successful integration through education and training of young people facing the greatest difficulties, irrespective of whether the action was taken at the initiative of the Member States, local authorities (regions or towns) or the business sector, and irrespective of whether or not they were part of a Community programme or initiative;
- to promote exchanges of experience and transnational projects in this context within the framework of a specific network infrastructure supported by the Commission.

This conference will provide an opportunity to bring together European expertise on school, social and occupational integration, to compare experiences already in progress or completed, and for the experts and political leaders to examine the conditions which need to be met to make a success of integrating young people in difficulty.

Programme

Day 1

Morning

9.30 a.m.	Reception and registration
10 a.m.–1 p.m.	Plenary session
Chairman:	Mr T. O'Dwyer, Director-General, DG XXII
Opening addresses:	Mrs Cresson, Member of the European Commission
Statement:	Karl-Johan Lönnroth, Director DG V.A.
Presentation of the aims of the conference:	Mr T. O'Dwyer, Director-General DG XXII

Keynote papers from studies undertaken in the framework of the action III.3.1 of Socrates 'Analysis of questions of common educational policy interest'

1. Dropping out and secondary education — Mr Massimiano Bucchi, IARD Research Institute (Italy)
2. Fostering educational success of socially excluded youngsters: from prevention to remedy — Mr Ides Nicaise, Catholic University of Leuven (Belgium). Case studies to be identified
3. Remedial strategies for failure at school in the EU: an overview and three case studies — Mr François-Marie Gérard, Bureau d'Ingénerie en Education et Formation (BIEF) (Belgium). Case studies to be presented: the ROC/RMC in the Netherlands, the workshop schools in Spain, the 'Velorep' project in Austria

1 p.m.–1.30 p.m.	Questions
1.30 p.m.–2.30 p.m.	*Lunch*

Afternoon

2.30 p.m.–5.30 p.m.	Topic workshops. First meeting: exchange of experience and identification of good practices
15.45–16.15	*Coffee break*

1. *What teaching methods for the integration of young people in difficulty? (Individualisation of pathways, active teaching methods, consideration of the achievements of experience, counselling and guidance, etc.)*

Speaker No 1:	Vejle kommunale Ungdomsskole in DHI. The integrated programme for people threatened with lifelong marginalisation — Eeva Sondergaard, Projektskolen Grennesminde (Denmark)
Speaker No 2:	Socrates basic skills project — David Horsburg, Basic skills project (United Kingdom)
Speaker No 3	Preventing exclusion at college level — Luarila Eeva, Helsinki Roihuvuori Vocational College (Finland)

Chairperson of the workshop: Christine Faucqueur, Ministry of Education (France)

2. *What role should the new technologies play?*

Speaker No 1:	Vocational education and guidance: New technologies — Christian Boldieu, Association Nationale pour la formation des adultes (AFPA) (France)
Speaker No 2:	New technologies in training programmes for disadvantaged young people in the city of Cologne (*Volkshochschule*) — Diethelm Jeske, AMT für Weiterbildung, Volkshochschule, Köln (Germany)
Speaker No 3:	New technologies: putting the learner in control — Bronwen Robinson, Lifeskills International Ltd (United Kingdom)

Chairperson of the workshop: Eddy Adams, Institute for Social and Economic Research, INSER, Glasgow (United Kingdom)

3. *Objectives and methods of validation and certification of skills*

Speaker No 1:	Objectives and methods for validation and certification of skills. UK case study: Rewarding and widening achievement: the ASDAN initiative — Dave Brockington, Award Scheme Development and Accreditation Network (ASDAN) (UK)
Speaker No 2:	Presentation of the Skills Portfolio approach used in training schemes for young school 'drop-outs' organised by the Integration Unit of the Aix-Marseille Education Authority — Joëlle Bruguiere, Aix-Marseille Education Authority, Daet Education Office, Ministry of Education Integration Unit (France)
Speaker No 3	The integration of young people into active life — Dr Maria Eugénia Santiago, Centro Social Paroquial Santo Antonio de Campolide (Portugal)

Chairperson of the workshop: Angela Lambkin, FAS (Ireland)

4. *How should trainers operate and what professional skills should they have? (Teaching team, tutoring and mentoring, training of trainers)*

Speaker No 1:	The training of tutors for social cooperatives forming part of vocational training and work induction projects for disadvantaged young people — Alain Goussot, CSAPSA, Centro studi analisi di psicologia e sociologia applicate (Italy)
Speaker No 2:	Teacher training. Why? — Miriam Diez Pinol, Centre d'Orientacío I Psicologica Aplicada (COPSA) (Spain)

Chairpersons of the workshop: Paul Forbes, Leeds Second Chance School (United Kingdom) and Ulrike Wisser, BBJ Servis (Germany)

5. *Participation of the company in training (objectives and arrangements)*

Speaker No 1   Experiences form the 'Qualified Helpers'scheme in Linz — Aloïs Reis-chl, Berufsschule Linz (Austria)

Speaker No 2:   Enterprise participation in training — Marie-Jo Sanchez, Centre d'Education et Formation en Alternance (CEFA), St Gilles (Belgium)

Speaker No 3:   Experiences in Italy particularly in the framework of the 'Law 44' and 'Informa Giovani' — Roberto Serra, SOLCO (Italy)

Chairperson of the workshop: Eneko Astigarraga, Prospektiker, Bilbao (Spain)

6. *How do actions fit into the local environment (integrated approach, multi-player partnership)?*

Speaker No 1:   How do actions fit into the local environment? A Youthreach perspective — Brigit Moylan, Youthreach Dublin (Ireland)

Speaker No 2:   Elefsina: An integrated local approach for the social and occupational integration of young people — Pinelopi Stathakopoulou, IEKEP (Greece)

Speaker No 3:   Villa Fridhem, Härnosand, Sweden — Orving Gunnar — Aurora Borealis (Sweden)

Speaker No 4:   Integrated training schemes — Laurent Wattelet, Ministry of Education Integration Unit, Lille (France)

Chairpersons of the workshop: Rudolf Mondelaers — Berufsfortbildungswerk (BFW), Berlin (Germany), and Victor Soares, Regional Development Agency of Setubal (Portugal)

Day 2

Morning

9.30–10.30 a.m.   Plenary session chaired by Mr Draxler, Director DG XXII.B

1. European coordination of the 'Second Chance School' pilot projects — Jean François Mézières, AFPA — DUE
2. European cooperation in the European virtual training college — Christoph Harnischmacher and Ulrich Rauter

10.30 a.m.   *Break*

11.00 a.m.–12.30 p.m.   Topic workshops. Second meeting: avenues for cooperation within the European network

Continuation of the topic workshops, the aim being to identify themes, approaches and methods of cooperation, joint projects, real or virtual exchanges, etc.

Workshop 1: *What teaching methods for the integration of young people in difficulty? (Individualisation of pathways, active teaching methods, consideration of the achievements of experience, counselling and guidance, etc.)*

Chairperson: Eeva Kaisa Linna, AIKE Inernational, network of Finnish Vocational Adult Education Centres (Finland)

Workshop 2: *What role should the new technologies play?*

Chairperson: Jacques Jansen, Centrum voor Europese Studies en Opleidingen (CESO) (Netherlands)

Workshop 3: *Objectives and methods of validation and certification?*

Chairperson: Clemes Romijn, University of Nijmegen (NL)

Workshop 4: *How should trainers operate and what professional skills should they have? (Teaching teams, tutoring and mentoring, training of trainers)*

Chairperson: Ulrike Wisser (BBJ Servis, D)

Workshop 5: *Participation of the company in training (objectives and arrangements).*

Chairperson: Jean Claude Bourcel, Second Chance School, Marseille (France)

Workshop 6: *How do actions fit into the local environment (integrated approach, multi-player partnership)?*

Chairperson: Vitor Soares, Setubal regional development agency (CDR) (Portugal)

12.30 p.m.	*Lunch*

Afternoon

2 p.m.–3 p.m.	Plenary session
Chairman:	Mr Domenico Lenarduzzi Director, DG XXII.A.

1. Summary of the thematic workshops 'second meeting' during which the rapporteurs highlight the themes, approaches and methods proposed for European level cooperation
2. If appropriate, presentation of cooperation projects which have already emerged within the network

3 p.m.	Round table *Action on the integration of young people*
Chairman:	Mr Domenico Lenarduzzi Director, DG XXII.A.

Introductory speech on a national perspective:

School failure and social exclusion of young persons — a challenge for policy-makers — the case of German'

Mr Haase, German Federal Ministry of Education, Science, Research and Technology

Participants:

- Commission
- Committee of the Regions: Dr John Evans;
- Economic and Social Committee: Mr Koryfidis.

4 p.m.	*End of proceedings* Mr Lenarduzzi *Director, DG XXII.A*

List of delegates
Brussels, 7 and 8 May

Integrating all young people into society
through education and training

Eddy Adams
INSER
44, Woodlands Street
G22 5QG Glasgow
United Kingdom
Tel. (44-141) 955 18 01
Fax (44-141) 955 18 02

Angélique Agyropoulou
Working Fellowship Organisation
Aghsilaou, 10
Athens
Greece
Tel. (30-1) 522 02 64
Fax (30-1) 524 61 89

Hannu Ahti
Alternative Vocational Institute
Haukilahdenkatu, 4
00550 Helsinki
Finland
Tel. (358-500) 50 89 97 - (358-9) 73 57 63
Fax (358-500) 73 57 63

Colin Ainsworth
AZTEC
2 Manorgate Road
KT2 7AL Kingston Upon Thames
United Kingdom
Tel. (44-181) 547 48 23
Fax (44-181) 547 38 84

Ludovico Albert
Comune di Torino
v. Palazzo di Città, 1
Torino
Italy
Tel. (39-11) 442 42 00
Fax (39-11) 560 64 14

Caroline Andries
European Committee of the International Reading Association
Vrije Universitteit Brussel Pleinlaan 2
Brussels
Belgium
Tel. (32-2) 629 25 28
Fax (32-2) 629 25 32

Eneko Astigarraga
Prospektiker
Don Leandro 3
20800 Zarautz
Spain
Tel. (34-94) 383 57 04
Fax (34-94) 313 25 20

Jane Ayshford
One Step Campden Institute
95 Lancaster Road
W11 1QQ London
United Kingdom
Tel. (44-171) 221 44 25
Fax (44-171) 221 07 27

François Banizette
Foyer Educatif Le Grand Cèdre
64, boulevard Alsace Lorraine
64000 Pau
France
Tel. (33-5) 59 30 26 07
Fax (33-5) 59 30 65 36

Bernard Basteyns
Sarbacane — CEFA
73, rue de la Croix de Pierre
1060 Brussels
Belgium
Tel. (32-2) 537 55 37
Fax (32-2) 537 55 37

Christy Berry
Rhondda Cynon Taff County Borough Council
The Pavillions Clydach Vale
CF40 2XX Rhondda
United Kingdom
Tel. (44-1443) 68 76 66
Fax (44-1443) 68 02 86

Marie Claude Betbeder
Le Monde Initiatives
Paris
France
Tel. (33-1) 39 11 12 97
Fax (33-1) 39 11 12 97

Jean Biarnes
UFR des Lettres et Sciences Humaines
avenue Jean-Baptiste Clément
93430 Villetaneuse
France
Tel. (33-1) 49 40 31 92
Fax (33-1) 49 40 37 06

Hans-Eugen Bierling Wagner
WUK
Wahringer Strasse 59
1090 Wien
Austria
Tel. (43-1) 401 21 74
Fax (43-1) 403 27 37

Cécile Bloch
Association: 'La Bouture' ex Lycée Elitaire pour
Tous
19, avenue Alsace Lorraine
38000 Grenoble
France
Tel. (33-4) 76 51 25 62
Fax (33-4) 76 51 25 62

Lars Blomgren
Second Chance Schools
Stockholmsvagen 35
60217 Norkoping
Sweden
Tel. (46-11) 15 33 93
Fax (46-11) 18 60 22

Patrice Blougorn
CNEFEI Suresnes
58/60, avenue des Landes
92150 Suresnes
France
Tel. (31-1) 41 44 31 21
Fax (31-1) 41 44 31 23

Christian Boeldieu
AFPA
3, allée du Muguet
60300 Apremont
France
Tel. (33-3) 44 24 29 74
Fax (33-3) 44 25 38 77

Jacques Bonnisseau
La Ville pour l'Ecole
393, rue de Vaugirard
75015 Paris
France
Tel. (33-1) 44 06 77 63
Fax (33-1) 44 06 77 63

Jean-Claude Bourcel
Ecole de la Deuxième Chance
82, avenue de la Croix Rouge
13013 Marseille
France
Tel. (33-4) 91 06 12 21
Fax (33-4) 91 66 58 66

Dave Brockington
ASDAN
6, Iddsleigh Road — Redland, Bristol
B86 6YF Bristol
United Kingdom
Tel. (44-117) 973 44 83
Fax (44-117) 973 09 18

Joëlle Bruguiere
Mission d'Insertion Aix-Marseille
Rectorat d'Aix Marseille
Place Lucien Paye
13100 Aix-en-Provence
France
Tel. (33-4) 42 91 70 65
Fax (33-4) 42 91 70 11

Massimiano Bucchi
IARD scrl — Istituto di Ricerca
via Soncino 1
Milano
Italy
Tel. (39-2) 869 21 77
Fax (39-2) 864 515 18

Averil Burgess
Youthreach Coordinator
Bray North Wicklow — Education
and Training Centre
Vevay Road
Ireland
Tel. (353-1) 286 95 98
Fax (353-1) 286 96 71

Gesualdo Carozza
Centro Europa per la Scuola Educazione
e Socita — CESES
via Roman sur Isère
21100 Varese
Italy
Tel. (39-2) 58 30 67 97 ou (39-332) 28 42 69
Fax (39-2) 58 30 38 00 ou (39-332) 28 42 69

Roxana Carvalho
00162 Rome
Italy
Tel. (39-347) 640 17 89
Fax (39-658) 194 53

Lucia Chiocchetti
Comune di Chieri
Via Palazzo di Città, 10
10023 Chieri
Italy
Tel. (39-11) 94 28 204
Fax (39-11) 94 70 250

Oliver Clancy
Fas Training Centre
Industrial Estate — Cork Road
Waterford
Ireland
Tel. (353-51) 30 15 12
Fax (353-51) 30 15 12

Pat Conway
FAS Training centre Garry Castle
Athlone
Ireland
Tel. (353-902) 751 28
Fax (353-902) 747 95

Maurice Cornil
Maison des Associations à Bruxelles
rue Haute, 88
1000 Brussels
Belgium
Tel. (32-2) 514 18 80
Fax (32-2) 514 00 66

Manuela Correia Lopes
Forpescas
Edificicio EPMC — Au Brasilia — Pedroucos
1400 Lisbon
Portugal
Tel. (351-1) 301 76 70
Fax (351-1) 301 64 82

Anne Cousin
Ministère de l'Education Nationale
107, rue de Grenelle
75357 Paris Cedex
France
Tel. (33-1) 55 55 22 60
Fax (33-1) 55 55 22 41

Christina Cramer
Raffviksvagen 103
16272 Vallingby
Sweden
Tel. (46-8) 706 85 67
Fax (46-8) 29 41 16

Dominique Croisier
AFPA Stains
70, bd Maxime Gorki - RN 301
93240 Stains
France
Tel. (33-1) 49 40 13 31
Fax (33-1) 49 40 13 69

Sandro Dal Piano
Enaip Veneto
Italy
Tel. (39-49) 864 47 58
Fax (39-49) 864 47 69

Robert Dekker
Dienst Stedelijk onderwijs
Postbox 70014

3000 Rotterdam
The Netherlands
Tel. (31-10) 417 34 69
Fax (31-10) 414 31 62

Marie-Françoise Delatour
Regione Emilio Romagna
Via Aldo Moro 38
40127 Bologna
Italy
Tel. (39-51) 28 38 80
Fax (39-51) 28 39 36

Renaud Demez
CEFA
Commune de Saint Gilles
73, rue de la Croix de Pierre
1060 Brussels
Belgium
Tel. (32-2) 537 55 37
Fax (32-2- 537 55 37

Jacques Deprez
Service Général des Affaires Pédagogiques
de la Recherche en Pédagogie et du Pilotage
de l'Enseignement organisé par la Communauté
européenne
Place Surlet de Chokier 15/17
1000 Brussels
Belgium

Stokes Dermot
Department of Education and Science — Irish
Life Centre
Block 4 — Talbot Street
Dublin 1
Ireland
Tel. (353-1) 872 92 93
Fax (353-1) 872 92 93

Miriam Diez Piñol
C.O.P.S.A.
Provença 122
08029 Barcelona
Spain
Tel. (34-3322) 08 88
Fax (34-3322) 10 05

John R. Evans
Committee of the Regions
United Kingdom
Fax (44-1685) 84 07 30

Caroline Farquhar
MBE Chief Executive
60, Brook Street
G40 2AB Bridgtown Glasgow
United Kingdom
Tel. (44-141) 556 19 91
Fax (44-141) 556 19 92

Christine Faucqueur
Ministère de l'Education
107, rue de Grenelle — DESCO A11
75007 Paris
France
Fax (33-1) 55 55 22 27

Paul Forbes
Leeds City Council
Training Department — Civic Hall Annexe
Leeds LS1 1UR West Yorkshire
United Kingdom
Fax (44-113) 2474311

Helen FRASER
Pilton Early Intervention Project
Holyrood Road
Edinburgh
United Kingdom
Tel. (44-131) 558 69 97
Fax (44-131) 558 64 09

Maria Emilia Galvão
Ministerio da Educacao
Av 5 de Outubro 107-7
1050 Lisboa
Portugal
Tel. (351-1) 793 42 54
Fax (351-1) 797 89 94

Mamen Garcia
Patronat Catale Pro Europa
227, rue de la Loi
1000 Brussels
Belgium
Tel. (32-2) 231 03 30
Fax (32-2) 230 21 10

Mercedes Garcia Del Estal
Escuela de la Segunda Oprtunidad de Barcelona
Paza d'espana 5, 5è
08014 Barcelona
Spain
Tel. (34-93) 318 78 79
Fax (34-93) 318 78 14

Agnès Georges
Association La Contine
153, rue du chemin de Chateau Lombert
13013 Marseille
France
Tel. (33-4) 91 95 96 01
Fax (33-4) 91 95 96 01

François-Marie Gérard
Bureau d'Ingénierie en Education
et en Formation
rue Rabelais17/101
1348 Louvain-la-Neuve
Belgium
Tel. (32-104) 528 46 20

Bernard Gerde
'La Bouture' ex Lycée Elitaire pour Tous
19, avenue Alsace Lorraine
38000 Grenoble
France
Tel. (33-4) 76 51 25 62
Fax (33-4) 76 51 25 62

Joost Geurts
Streekgeweest Oostelijk Zuid Limburg
Postbus 200
6400 AE Heerlen
The Netherlands
Tel. (31-45) 571 88 20
Fax (31-45) 574 09 08

Simon Goldberg
FOREM
104, boulevard Tirou
6000 Charleroi
Belgium
Tel. (32-70) 20 61 52
Fax (32-70) 20 61 99

Alain Goussot
CAPSA
Via Marsala, 30
40126 Bologna
Italy
Tel. (39-51) 23 04 49
Fax (39-51) 23 14 40

Claudel Guitard
Service de Pédagogie Experimentale
15, avenue des Tilleuls
4000 Liège
Belgium
Tel. (32-4) 366 94 95
Fax (32-4) 366 91 45

Hernn Haase
General Education, Vocational Education and
Training
Federal Ministry of Education
Heinemannstrasse 2
53170 Bonn
Germany

Ole Hansen
Denmark
Tel. (45-86) 98 77 55
Fax (45-86) 98 57 05

Nathalie Harar
Service Social des Jeunes — Centre de Formation
— Antenne Emploi
27, avenue de Ségur
75007 Paris
France
Tel. (33-1) 47 83 66 95
Fax (33-1) 40 56 31 32

Christophe Harnischmacher
IMBSE
Im Moerser Feld, 1
47441 Moers
Germany
Tel. (49-2841) 91 73 20
Fax (49-2841) 91 73 26

H. Hawlicek
Austria

Ascan Heuwold
IB Dormagen
Hackhauser Strasse 63
41640 Dormagen
Germany
Tel. (49-2133) 636 52–606 43
Fax (49-2133) 26 99 10

David Horsburgh
Lewisham College
Lewisham Way
London SE4 1UT
United Kingdom
Tel. (44-181) 694 32 71
Fax (44-181) 694 91 63

Marjaleena Hulkko
Vocational Adult Educational Centre
Hattelmalantie 25
13101 Hameenlinna
Finland
Tel. (358-3) 614 75 21
Fax (358-3) 614 75 55

Eileen Humphreys
Athens Second Chance School
10 Grosvenor Gardens
London
United Kingdom
Tel. (44-171) 411 43 00
Fax (44-171) 411 43 01

Javier Ibáñez
CES Proyecto Hombre Madrid
c/ Martin de los Heros
28008 Madrid
Spain
Tel. (34-91) 542 35 07
Fax (34-91) 542 46 93

Lourdes Ibáñez do Galiva
Pesidenta
Manola Qojario, 9
Madrid
Spain
Tel. (34-91) 797 69 55
Fax (34-91) 798 43 51

Rosa Iglesias
Agencia Local de Promocion Economica
y Empleo
Ayuntamiento de Gijon
33207 Gijon
Spain
Tel. (34-985) 17 12 84
Fax (34-985) 17 21 02

Jacques Jansen
CESO
St Maartenslaan 26
6221 AX Maastricht
The Netherlands
Tel. (31-43) 350 01 55
Fax (31-43) 350 02 68

Diethelm Jeske
Beruftigunfördernde Weiterbildund
Josef Haubrich Hof 2
50676 Köln
Germany
Tel. (49-221) 221 36 80
Fax (49-221) 221 63 30

Roland Kastler
Mission d'Insertion Aix-Marseille
Rectorat d'Aix-Marseille
Place Lucien Paye
13100 Aix en Provence
France
Tel. (33-4) 42 91 70 65
Fax (33-4) 42 91 70 11

Anneli Kellberg
EKAKS
Malminginkatu 6 PL 52
48601 Karhula
Finland
Tel. (358-5) 234 55 77
Fax (358-5) 234 55 82

Helen Keogh
Vocational training Opportunities Scheme
Sundrive Road
Dublin 12
Ireland
Tel. (353-1) 453 54 87
Fax (353-1) 453 76 59

Lars Kjeldahl
Ella & Moller Sorigs Fond
Brodslevvejen 15
9480 Lokken
Denmark
Tel. (45-98) 88 30 10
Fax (45-98) 88 30 10

Raphael Kneip
Action Sociale pour les Jeunes
BP 5027
1050 Luxembourg
Luxembourg
Tel. (352-43) 90 66 1
Fax(352-43) 90 66 80

Effrossini KOUNTIOU
AFPA — Montreuil
France

Jan Kovarovic
Educational Policy Centre
Myslikova 7
Praha
Czech Republic
Tel. 420
Fax 420 22 49 10 515

Alessandra La Marca
Associazione ARCES
Via Lombardia 6
90144 Palermo
Italy
Tel. (39-91) 34 66 29
Fax (39-91) 34 63 77

Liliane Lafond
AFPA — Montreuil
France

J.M. Lahbouz
AFPA — Montreuil
France

Livio Lai
AFPA — Montreuil
France

Angela Lambkin
FAS
27-33 Upper Baggot Street
Dublin 4
Ireland
Tel. (353-1) 607 09 27
Fax (353-1) 607 06 07

Reinhard Lange - Koppel
WBZ Arbeit und Leben
Handelsplatz, 1
04439 Engelsdorf
Germany
Tel. (49-341) 656 47 16
Fax (49-341) 656 47 33

Charles Laplanche
Comité Intercommunal pour le Développement
et l'Emploi
1 rue du Moulin
Schifflange
Luxembourg
Tel. (352-53) 04 45 21
Fax (352-53) 04 45 41

Thorkild Larsen
Karup Danish Blue Cross Blue College
Liflevej 14
8600 Silkeborg
Denmark
Tel. (45-86) 81 15 00
Fax (45-86) 82 96 70

Hardy Laue
Akadelie Uberlingen
Magdebourg
Germany
Tel. (32-2) 375 98 23
Fax (32-2) 374 22 00

Eeva Laurila
Helsinki Roihuvuori Vocational College
Prinsessantie 2
00820 Helsinki
Finland
Tel. (358-9) 31 08 47 01
Fax (358-9) 31 08 47 10

Emilio Lazaro Blanco
Associacion Semilla
c/Paseo de Talleres 56
28021 Madrid
Spain
Tel. (34-1798) 69 55
Fax (34-1797) 48 19

Eija Leinonen
Kotka Vocational Adult Education Centre
Po Box 52
48601 Karhula
Finland
Tel. (358-5) 234 55 75
Fax (358-5) 234 55 82

Isabel Maria Leitao
Santa Casa de Misericordia de Sintra
Praceta 25 de Abril
2710 Sintra
Portugal
Tel. (351-1) 924 15 46
Fax (351-1) 923 92 78

Jorgen Lindholm
CSEE ETUCE
155, boulevard Emile Jacqemain
1210 Brussels
Belgium
Tel. (32-2) 224 06 92
Fax (32-2) 224 02 94

Eeva-Kaisa Linna
AIKE International
Kruunuvuorenkatu 5c15
00160 Helsinki
Finland
Tel. (358-9) 75 11 51 25
Fax (358-9) 75 11 51 27

Frank Lohmann
Betriehschatenleiter Berufsausbildungwerk
Helmholzstr. 1-3
10787 Berlin
Germany
Tel. (49-30) 493 28 39
Fax (49-30) 391 30 46

John Loodts
Communauté Française de Belgique
45, boulevard Reyer
1030 Brussels
Belgium
Tel. (32-2) 735 88 45
Fax (32-2) 735 88 45

Mackle Mairead
Advanced Learning Systems
Kennedy Way
Belfast BT11 9OT
United Kingdom
Tel. (44-1232) 61 66 81
Fax (44-1232) 60 12 13

Najem Maleke
Mitarbeiter der Geschaftsstelle Auslanderbeirat
Tieglstrasse 2
45141 Essen
Germany
Tel. (49-201) 888 85 29
Fax (49-201) 888 85 27

Natacha Martynow
Service de Pédagogie Experimentale
15, avenue des Tilleuls
4000 Liège
Belgium
Tel. (32-4) 366 94 95
Fax (32-4) 366 91 45

John Mc Carthy
Community Based Guidance Assistance
National Centre for Guidance in Education
Dublin
Ireland
Tel. (353-1) 873 14 11
Fax (353-1) 873 13 16

Maria Deonilde Mendes Almeida
Ministère de l'Education du Portugal
Lisbonne
Portugal
Tel. (351-1) 497 01 02
Fax (351-1) 497 11 13

Jean-François Mézières
AFPA — Montreuil
France

Jean-François Mingot
Institut Jean Errecart
64120 Saint Palais
France
Tel. (33-5) 59 65 70 77
Fax (33-5) 59 65 94 52

Rudolf Mondelaers
Berufsortbildungswerk GmbH
Keithstrasse 1-3
10787 Berlin
Germany
Tel. (49-30) 211 80 54
Fax (49-30) 211 86 54

Celia Moore
IBM UK
United Kingdom
Tel. (44-171) 202 31 87
Fax (44-171) 261 08 16

Briget Moylan
Youthreach Coordinator Dublin
Sundrive Road Crumlin D12
Ireland
Tel. (353-1) 623 10 55
Fax (353-1) 623 56 17

John Nash
Devon & Cornwall New Start Partnership
205, Creakavose Park
St Austell Cornwall PL26 7ND
United Kingdom
Tel. (44-1726) 82 46 08
Fax (44-1726) 82 40 88

Marie-Claire Neill-Cowper
Committe of the Regions
Belgium

Brigitta Nenzen
Ecole de Solna
Rostavagen 25
16954 Solna
Sweden
Tel. (46-8) 734 28 01
Fax (46-8) 734 26 38

Ides Nicaise
HIVA — Univ Leuven
Van Evenstraat 2E
3000 Leuven
Belgium
Tel. (32-16) 32 33 37
Fax (32-16) 32 33 44

Gus O'Connell
National Youth Federation
27-33 Upper Baggot St
Dublin 4
Ireland
Tel. (353-1) 607 05 92 or 00
Fax (353-1) 607 06 28

Jukka Onttonen
Oma Ura/My Own Carieer
Kotokuja 2
70780 Kuopio
Finland
Tel. (358-50) 569 11 66
Fax (358-17) 18 44 60

Gunnar Orving
Aurora Borealis
Kyrkgatan 4
96133 Boden
Sweden
Tel. (46-611) 277 50
Fax (46-921) 527 51

Ojvind Ottesen
Ella & Moller Sorigs Fond
Brodslevvejen 15
9480 Lokken
Denmark
Tel. (45-98) 88 30 10
Fax (45-98) 88 30 10

Jeana Papmichail
John Weathley College
1346 Shettleson Road
Glasgow G32 9AT
United Kingdom
Tel. (44-141) 778 84 26
Fax(44-141) 771 03 51

Ana Pardo Lopez Abad
Ministerio de Educacion y Cultura
Argumosa, 43
28012 Madrid
Spain
Tel. (34-1) 506 54 86
Fax (34-1) 429 77 88

Enrique Parilla
UPE de Sevilla
Pabelon Real Plaza de America s/n
41013 Sevilla
Spain
Tel. (34-95) 459 09 38
Fax (34-95) 459 09 03

Jenny Parker
Torfaen County Borough Council

Celia Pereira
CDR
Parque Industrial SAPEC
2900 Setubal
Portugal
Tel. (351-65) 53 45 50
Fax (351-65) 53 47 20

Ettore Piazza
IPSCT Don Zeffirino Jodi
Via Canalina, 21/1
42100 Reggio Emilia
Italy
Tel. (39-522) 32 57 11
Fax (39-522) 29 42 33

Caroline Pickering
North of England Office
Avenue de Broqueville 3
1150 Brussels
Belgium
Tel. (32-2) 735 35 47
Fax (32-2) 735 40 74

Raffaele Porta
Provincia di Napoli
Assessore Alle Politichi
Piazza Matteotti 1
Napoli
Italy
Tel. (39-81) 794 92 13 — (39-81) 551 87 69
Fax (39-81) 551 87 69

Lydia Pott
IFPE Gummersbach
Friedrichsfaler str 39
51645 Gummersbach
Germany
Tel. (49-2261) 98 97 11
Fax (49-2261) 98 97 60

Katerina Poutou
Arsis
15, K Loukareos
11475 Athens
Greece
Tel. (30-1) 644 21 98
Fax (30-1) 644 21 98 or 642 46 03

Giuseppe Quinto
60, rue du Marché
59000 Lille
France
Tel. (33-3) 20 78 21 13
Fax (33-3) 20 93 97 01

Pirjo Ranta
Educational and Cultural Affairs
City Hall — PB 205
48101 Kotka
Finland
Tel. (358-5) 234 53 96
Fax (358-5) 234 53 85

Alois Reischl
Berufsschule Linz 7
Ferihumerstrasse 28
4040 Linz
Austria
Tel. (43-732) 73 30 36
Fax (43-732) 73 30 36

Brownen Robinson
Lifskills International
United Kingdom
Tel. (44-1943) 85 10 51
Fax (44-1943) 85 12 40

Paul Roper
Brent Council — Education Service
9 Park Lane
Wembley Middx. HA9 7RW
United Kingdom
Tel. (44-181) 937 31 11
Fax (44-181) 201 31 72

Maciej Rozanski
Szkot Ogolnoksztatcacych
Stupsk ul Adama Mickiewicza 32
Slupsk
Poland
Tel. (48-59) 42 48 94
Fax (48-59)

Norbert Ruepert
Utrecht College Regionales Ausbildungszentrum
Livingstonelaan 609
3526 HL Utrecht
The Netherlands
Tel. (31-302) 87 77 00
Fax (31-302) 88 38 99

Marie-Jo Sanchez
CEFA
Commune de Saint Gilles
73, rue de la Croix de Pierre
1060 Brussels
Belgium
Tel. (32-2) 537 55 37
Fax (32-2) 537 55 37

Maria Eugenia Santiago
Centro Paroquial Santo Antonio de Campolide
Bairro da Serafina
1070 Lisboa
Portugal
Tel. (351-138) 86 19 02
Fax (351-138) 829 43

Klaus Schlik
Bundesministerium fur Unterricht
Minoritenplatz 5
1041 Wien
Austria
Tel. (43-1) 53 10 20 23 71
Fax (43-1) 531 20 22 92

Kristina Schmidt
Arbeittervoorfahrt Kreisverband Hannover Stadt
Marienstrasse 14
30171 Hannover
Germany
Tel. (49-511) 285 54 25
Fax (49-511) 285 54 30

Arno Scholten
ISB Institut für Schulung und Beruf
Wilhelm-Mangel Strasse, 17-19
56410 Montabaur
Germany
Tel. (49-2602) 90 65 00
Fax (49-2602) 906 50 50

Helmuth Schweitzer
Regional Arbeitsstelle
Tieglestr. 27
45141 Essen
Germany
Tel. (49-201) 832 84 01
Fax (49-201) 832 83 33

Hernn Sejdel
Senatsverwaltung fur Schule, Jugend und Sport
Storkower Str 133
10407 Berlin
Germany
Tel. (49-30) 42 14 46 57
Fax (49-30) 42 14 40 06

Roberto Serra
Solco Brescia
via Castellini, 9
25123 Brescia
Italy
Tel. (39-30) 29 79 62 24
Fax (39-30) 29 05 07

Lawrence Silwyn
Neath and Port Talbot Borough Council
Miland Road — Neath, Wales
United Kingdom
Tel. (44-1639) 63 64 67
Fax (44-1639)64 65 79

Stuart Smith
KCC
Springfield, Maidstone
Kent
United Kingdom
Tel. (44-1622) 69 65 54
Fax (44-1622) 69 49 71

Vitor Soares
CDR
Parque Industrial SAPEC
2900 Setubal
Portugal
Tel. (351-65) 53 45 50
Fax (351-65) 53 47 20

Hending Soerensen
Vejle Kommunale Ungdomsskole — DHI/PGU
— Vejle
Enghavevej 34
7100 Vejle
Denmark
Tel. (45-75) 72 72 99
Fax (45-75) 72 71 99

Blanca Soler
Patronat Catale Pro Europa
227, rue de la Loi
1000 Brussels
Belgium
Tel. (32-2) 231 03 30
Fax (32-2) 230 21 10

Eva Søndergaard
Vejle Kommunale Ungdomsskole — DHI/PGU
— Vejle
Enghavevej 34
7100 Vejle
Denmark
Tel. (45-75) 72 72 99
Fax (45-75) 72 71 99

Agusto Souza
Plan Individuel de Formation, Prévention de
l'échec scolaire
Penteado
2860 Moita
Portugal
Tel. (351-1) 238 13 08
Fax (351-1) 236 32 86

Carlo Ennio Stasi
Nuova Comunicazione SRL
Italien Largo R. Lanciani 24
I-00162 Roma
Italy
Tel. (39-68) 621 12 59
Fax (39-68) 60 03 08

Pinelopi Stathakopoulou
IEKEP Institute of Training and Vocational
Guidance

19, Kritis Street
15122 Athens
Greece
Tel. (30-1) 21 86 971/0
Fax (30-1) 21 86 972

Eugenie Stavropoulou
Département de la Formation Professionnelle
Initiale
Greece
Tel. (30-1)
Fax (30-1) 998 96 86

Phil Street
CEDC Woodway Park School
Wingston Road
CV2 2RH Coventry
United Kingdom
Tel. (44-1203) 65 57 00
Fax (44-1203- 65 57 01

Helen Theodoropoulos
National Labour Institute
K. Palama 6-8
11141 Athens
Greece
Tel. (30-1) 211 21 56
Fax (30-1) 228 51 22

John Thurlbeck
City of Sunderland — European Team
Civic Center
SR2 7DN Sunderland
United Kingdom
Tel. (44-191) 553 11 58
Fax (44-191) 55 31 19

Eva Torok
Hungarian Mission to the EU
44 avenue du Vert Chasseur
1040 Brussels
Belgium
Tel. (32-2) 372 08 80
Fax (32-2) 372 07 84

Tuuli Tuomi
Turku City Municipal — Youth Affairs
Linnankatu 61
20100 Turku
Finland
Tel. (358-50) 554 63 74
Fax (358-2) 231 93 74

Georges Ulbachs
Maecon
Postbus 306
6400 AH Heerlen

The Netherlands
Tel. (31-45) 560 55 55
Fax (31-45) 560 55 60

Jan Van Putten
Onderwijsgroep Haaglanden
Sammersveg 2
2285 SB Rijswijk
The Netherlands
Tel. (31-70) 32 98 901
Fax (31-70) 32 10 308

Marco Vinante
IARD scrl — Istituto di Ricera
via Soncino 1
Milano
Italy
Tel. (39-2) 869 21 77
Fax (39-2) 86 45 15 18

Panayota Vorloov
Institute for Continuing Adult Education —
IDEKE
60 Mitropoleos Street
10563 Athens
Greece
Tel. (30-1) 33 14 93 15
Fax (30-1) 331 49 30

Maya Vos
Onderwijsgroep Haaglanden
Sammersveg 2
2285 SB Rijswijk
The Netherlands
Tel. (31-70) 329 89 01
Fax (31-70) 321 03 08

Joan Walsh
Area Development Management Ltd
Holbrook House — Holles Street
Dublin 2
Ireland
Tel. (353-1) 661 36 11
Fax (353-1) 661 04 11

Laurent Wattelet
Mission Générale Insertion — Académie de Lille
Apart 122 Résidence Mandela
328 rue du 8 mai
59490 Somain
France
Tel. (33-3) 20 15 60 68
Fax (33-3) 20 15 66 04

Ulrich Wisser
BBJ-EU-News
65, rue de la Pacification

1000 Brussels
Belgium
Tel. (32-2) 230 41 45
Fax (32-2) 230 94 51

Chris Yapp
ICL lifelong Learning
2, Illingworth Close — Bramley Hants
Tadley
United Kingdom
Tel. (44-134) 447 20 01
Fax (44-134) 447 27 47

Martin Yarnit
Sheffield Education Service

Leopold Street
S1 1RJ Sheffield
United Kingdom
Tel. (44-114) 273 63 65
Fax (44-114) 273 62 79 or 258 50 08

Avelina Zorilla Torras
Ministerio de Eucacion y Cultura
Coordinadora del Programa Socrates-Comenius-
Accion 2
Los Madrazo 17
28071 Madrid
Spain
Tel. (34-1) 531 45 30
Fax (34-1) 522 70 48

European Commission

Integrating all young people into society through education and training
Volume 1 — Proceedings of the meeting — Brussels, 7 and 8 May 1998

Luxembourg: Office for Official Publications of the European Communities

2000 — 178 pp. — 21 x 29.7 cm

Volume I: ISBN 92-828-7632-2
Volume I and II: ISBN 92-828-7630-6